Puzzle Pals

Bryce Ross

Alles Zeichnen Lernen

Bryce Ross

ISBN: 978-1-990100-75-8

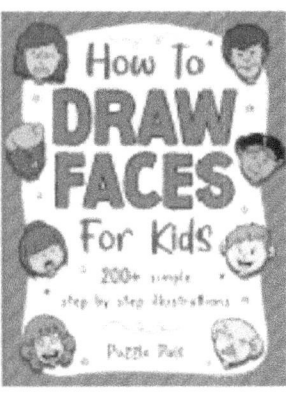

Leopard Übung

Giraffe Übung

Nilpferd Übung

Tiger Übung

Löwe Übung

Elefant Übung

Kuh

Ochse

Schwein

Schaf

Lama

Ziege

Kaninchen

Biber

Maulwurf

Huhn

Ente

Truthahn

Igel

Meerschweinchen

Eichhörnchen

Kätzchen Übung

Welpe Übung

Hamster Übung

Dschinn

Gartenzwerg

Monster

Yeti

Sasquatch

Troll

Lemur

Erdmännchen

Stinktier

Koala

Faultier

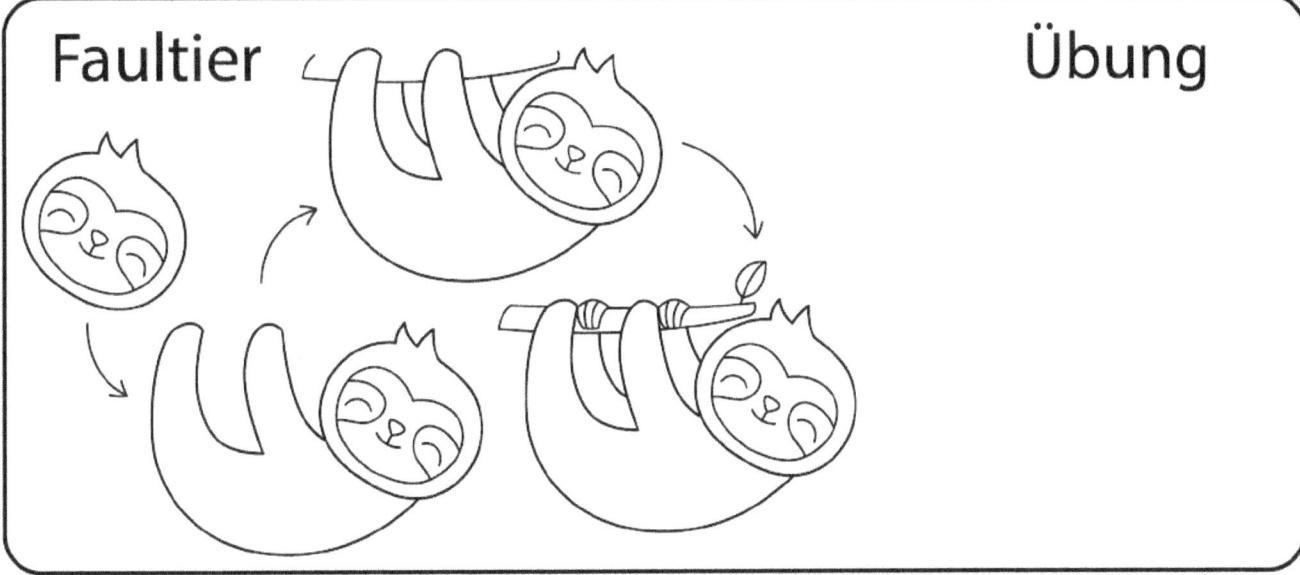

Panda

Hirsch

Kamel

Känguru

Fledermaus Übung

Maus Übung

Frettchen Übung

Wurm

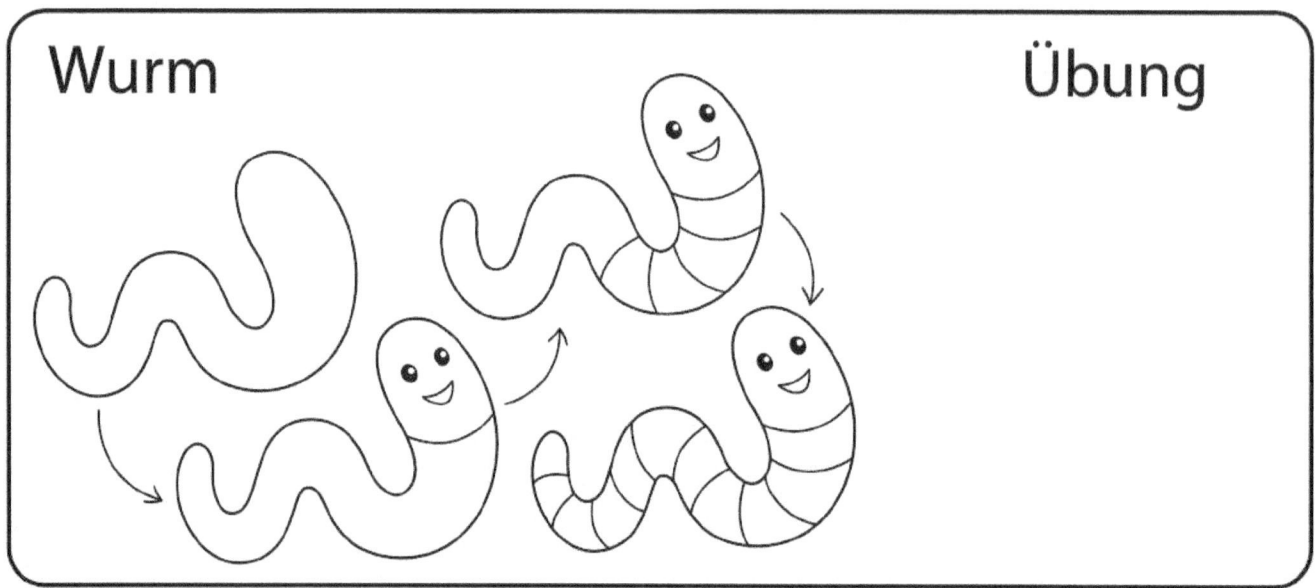

Schlange

Kröte

Biene

Schmetterling

Libelle

Heuschrecke

Marienkäfer

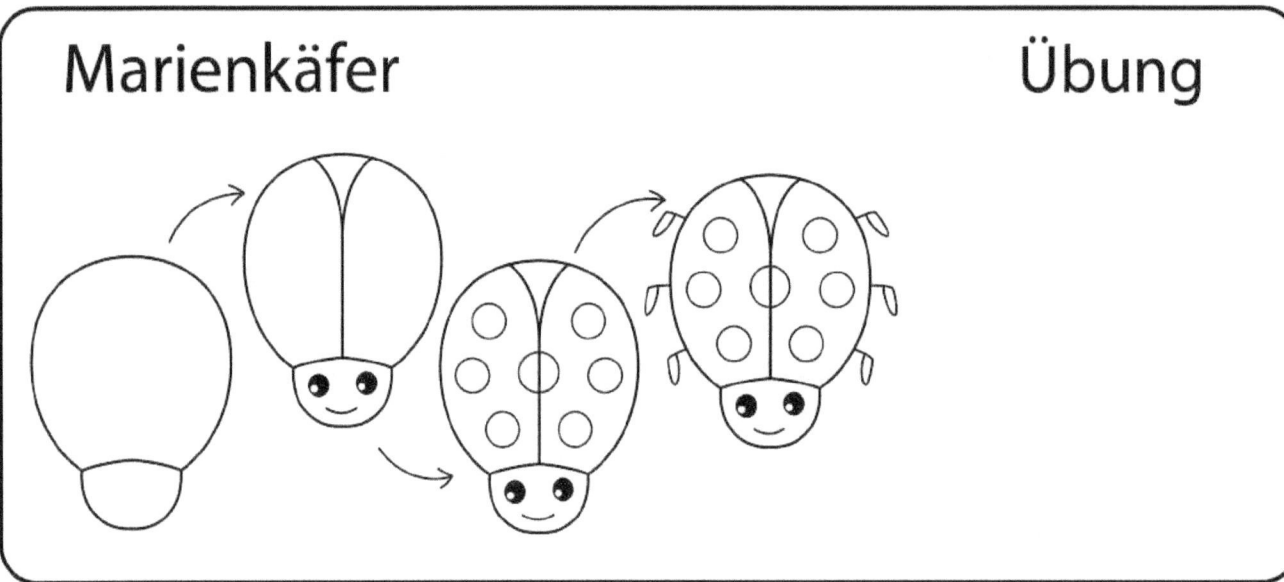

Spinne

Chamäleon

Eidechse

Alligator

Frosch

Schildkröte

Schnecke

Zebra   Übung

Pferd   Übung

Esel   Übung

Pinguin Übung

Robbe Übung

Seelöwe Übung

Delfin Übung

Hai Übung

Wal Übung

Kugelfisch

Seestern

Fisch

Krabbe Übung

Goldfisch Übung

Oktopus Übung

Eule

Tukan

Flamingo

Rabe

Papagei

Möwe

Gorilla Übung

Schimpanse Übung

Grizzlybär Übung

Otter

Gürteltier

Fuchs

Schildkröte

Kröte

Käfer

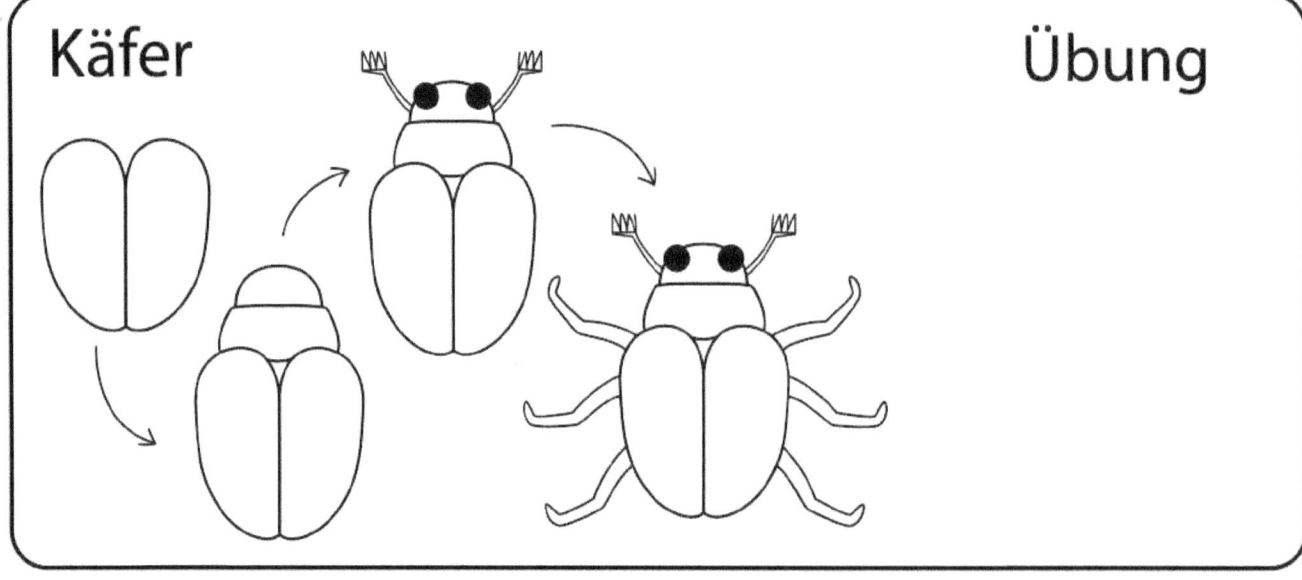

Katze

Hund

Waschbär

Raumschiff Übung

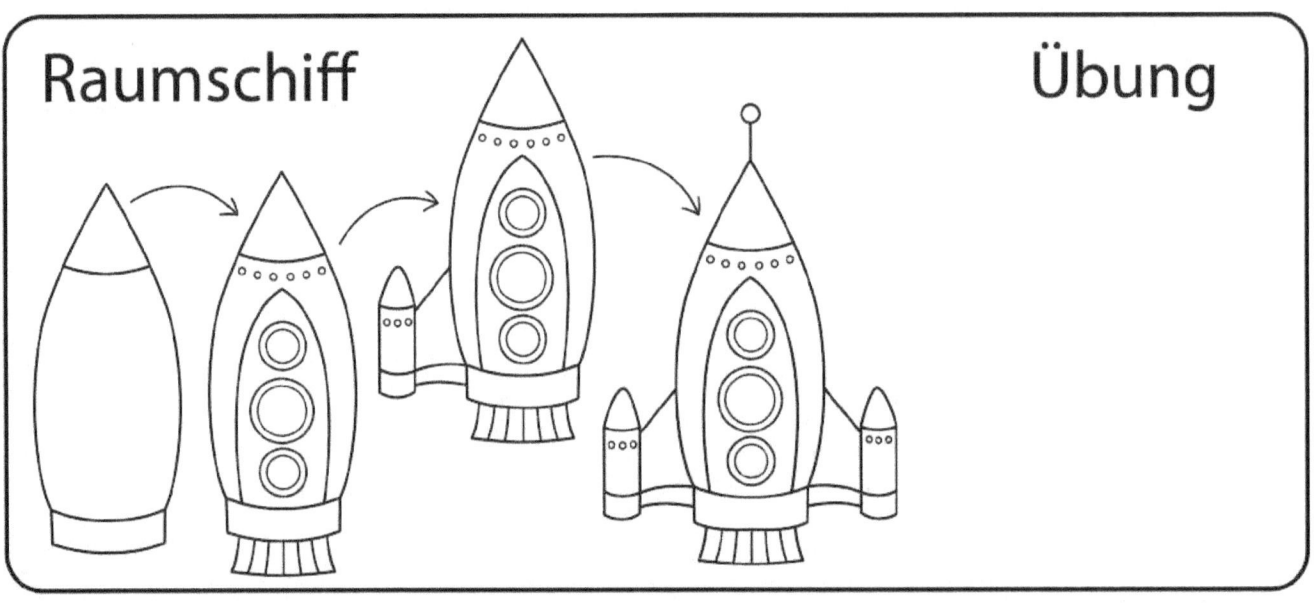

Raumschiff Übung

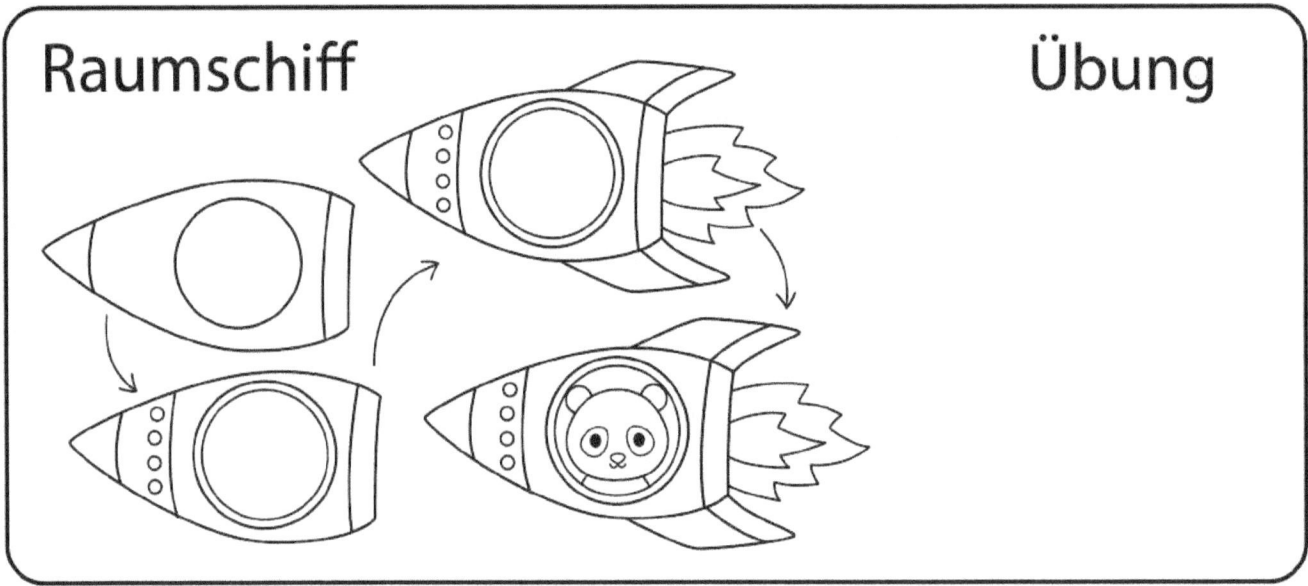

Raumschiff Übung

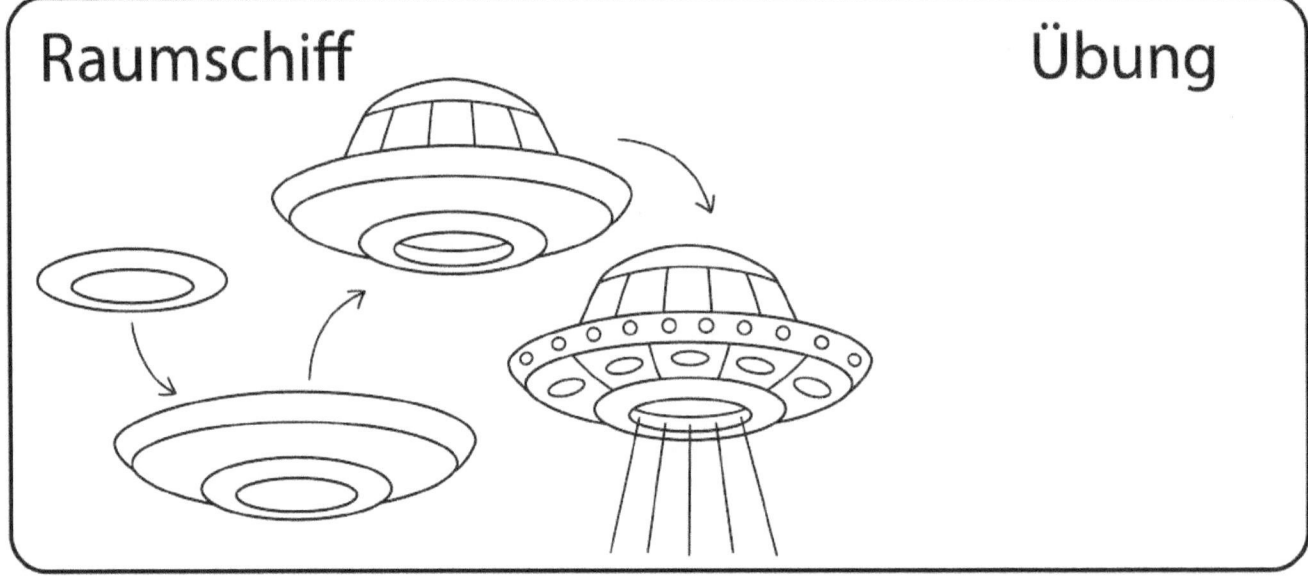

Roboter Übung

Roboter Übung

Roboter Übung

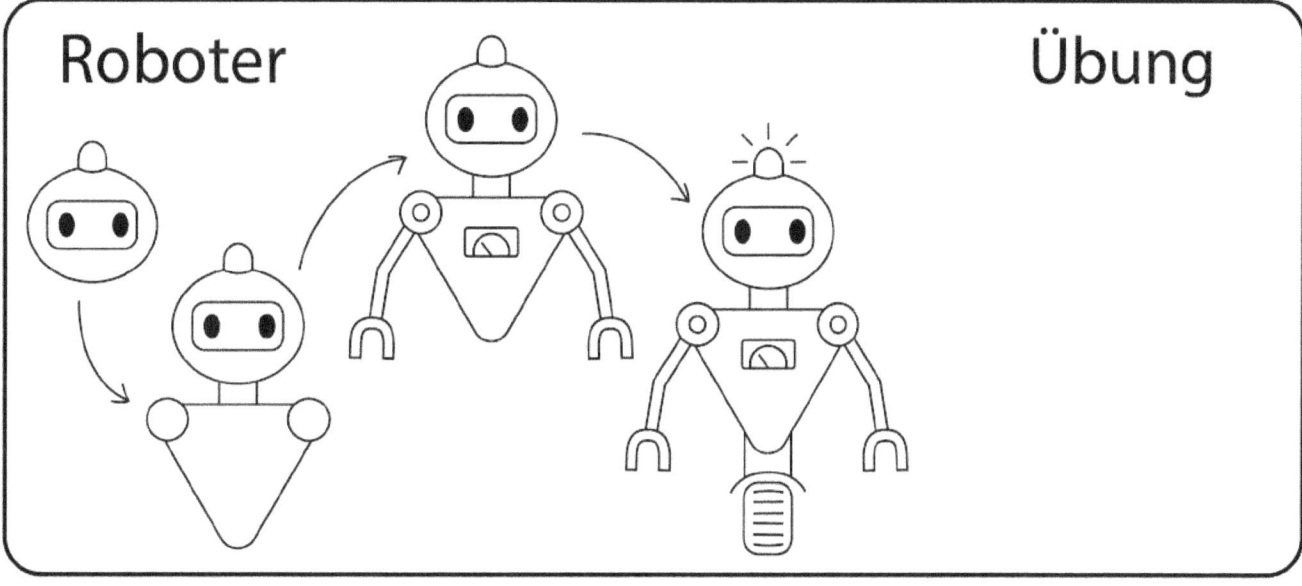

Raumschiff

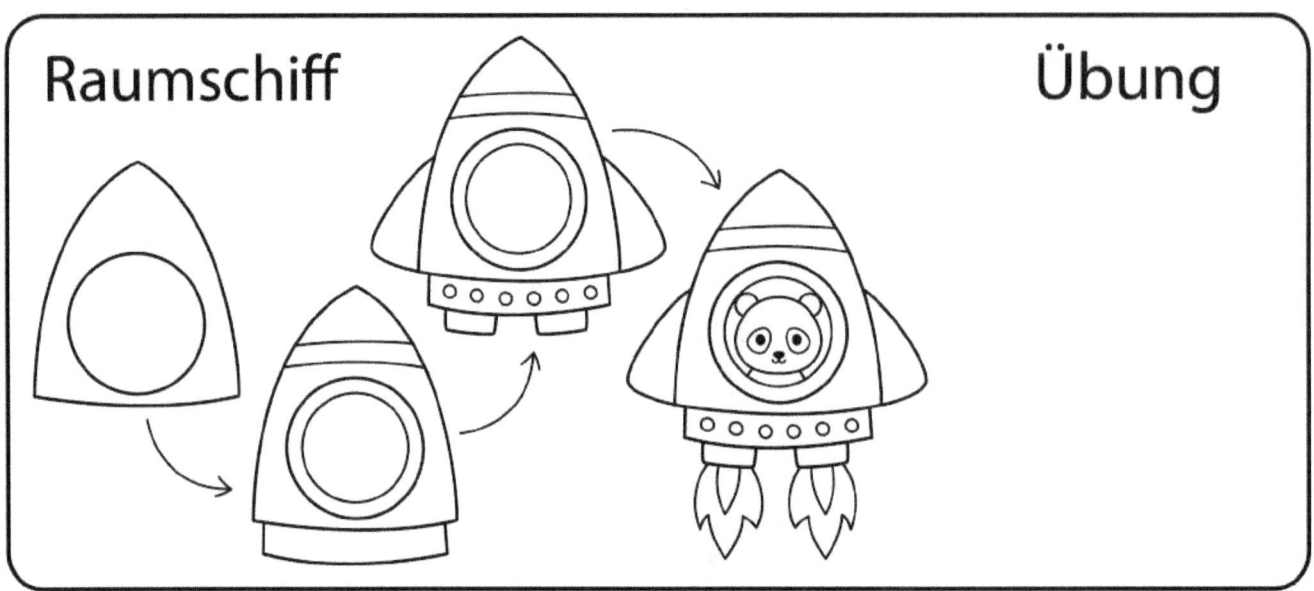

Astronauten-Katze

Astronauten-Fuchs

Raumschiff

Alien-Raumschiff

Astronaut

Alien-Raumschiff

Raumschiff

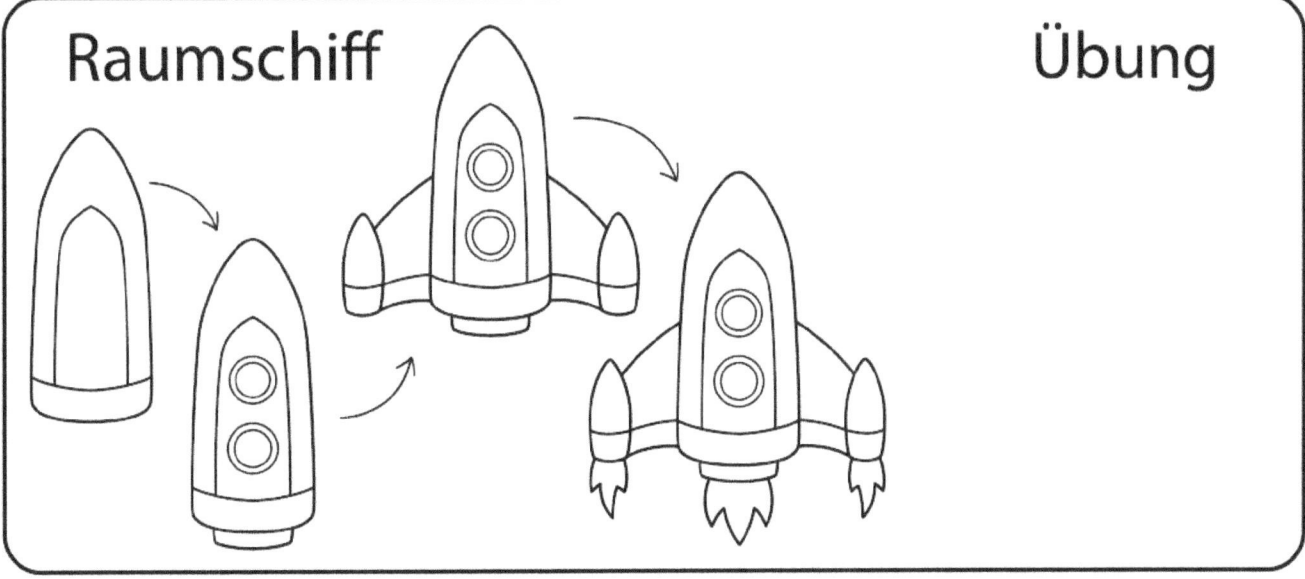

Mars-Rover

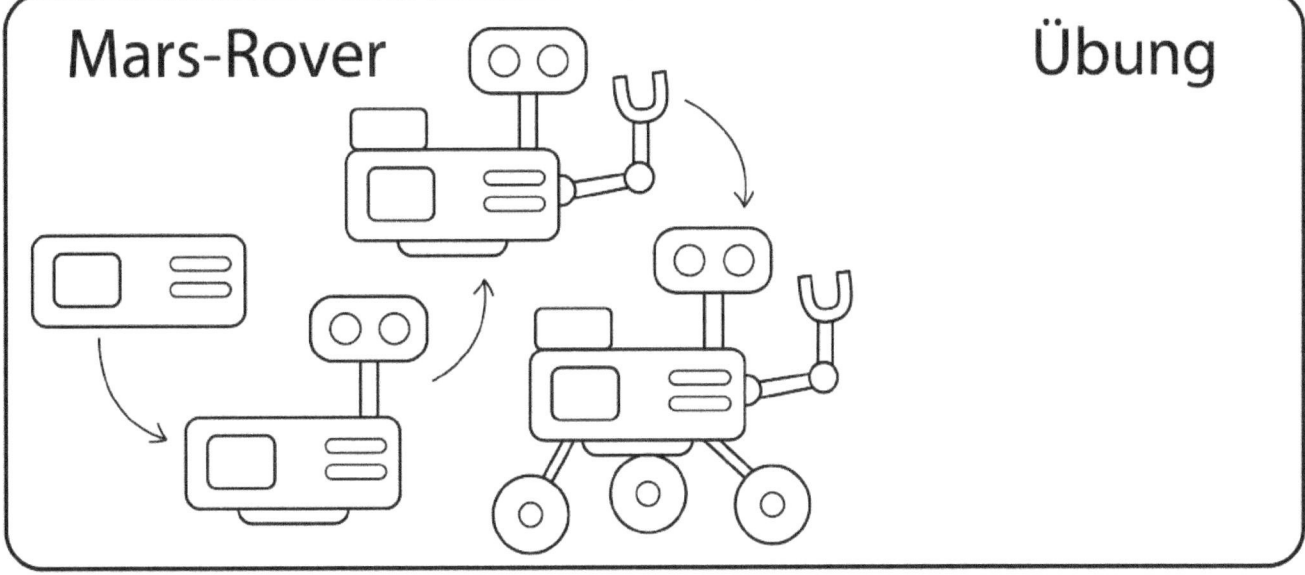

Satellit

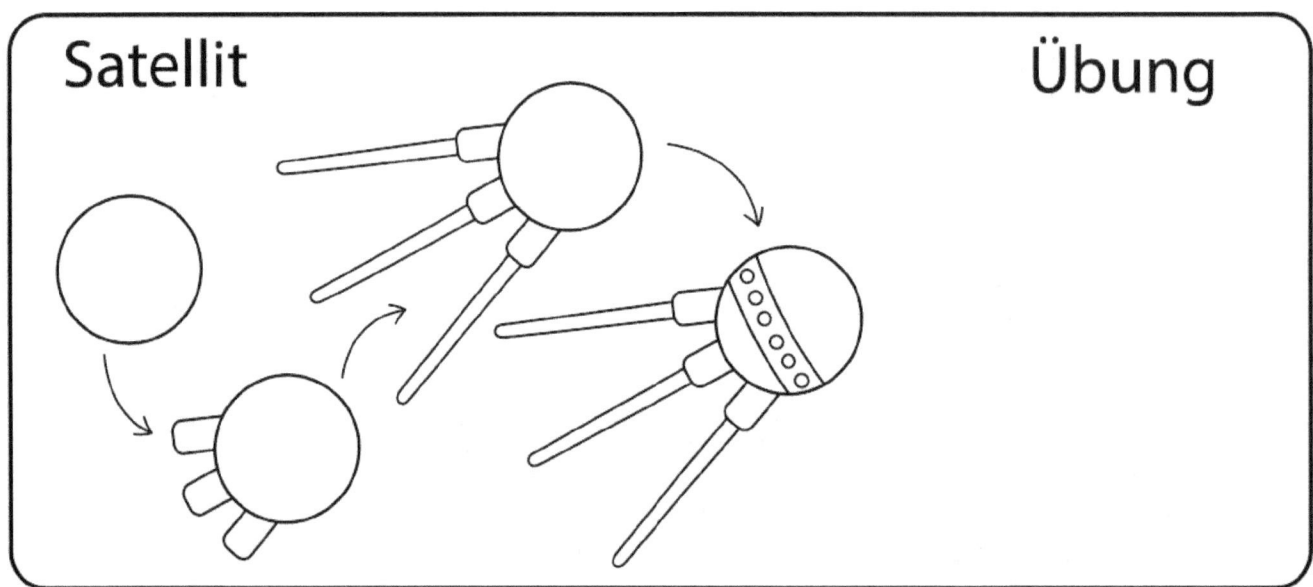

Raumstation

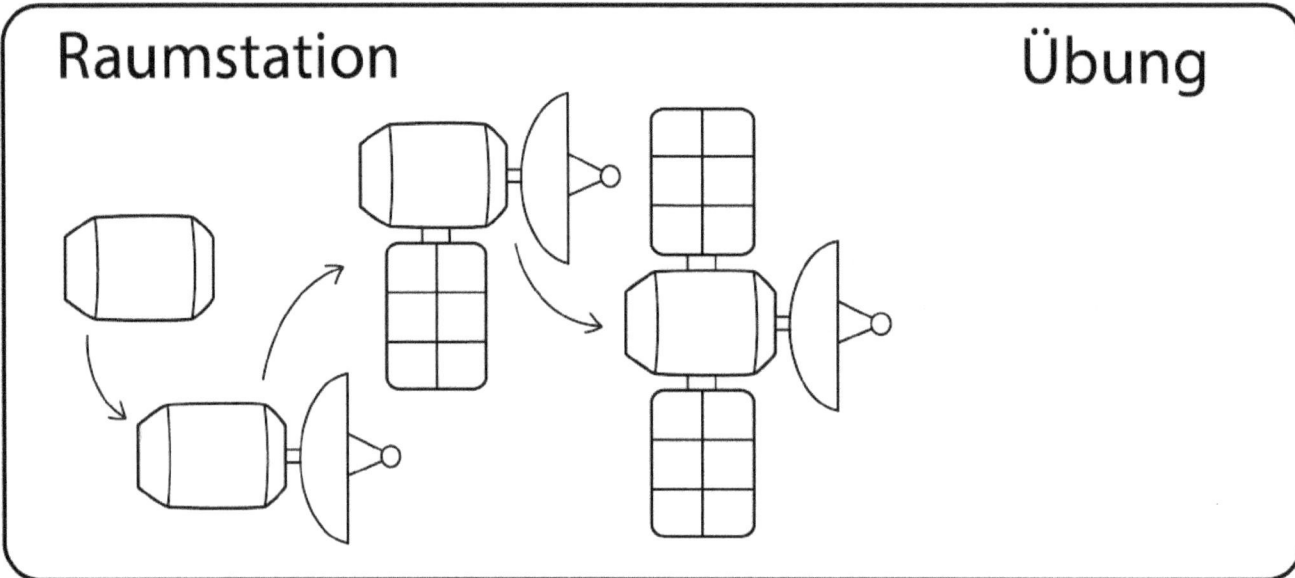

Meteorit

Die Erde

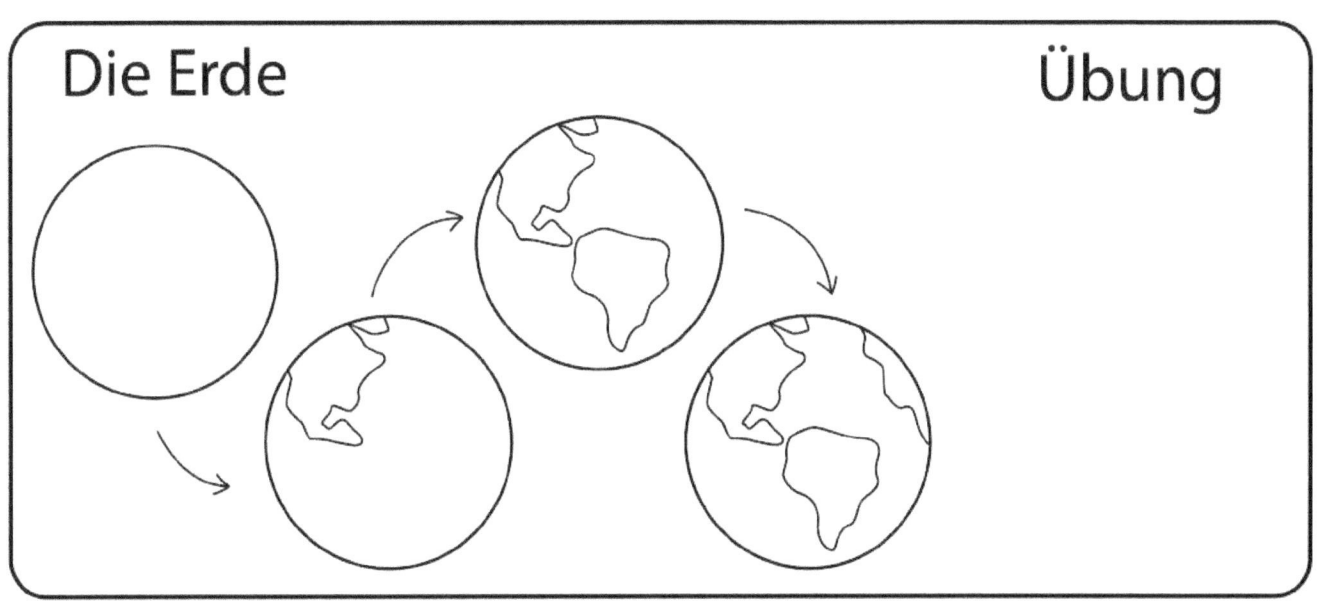

Saturn

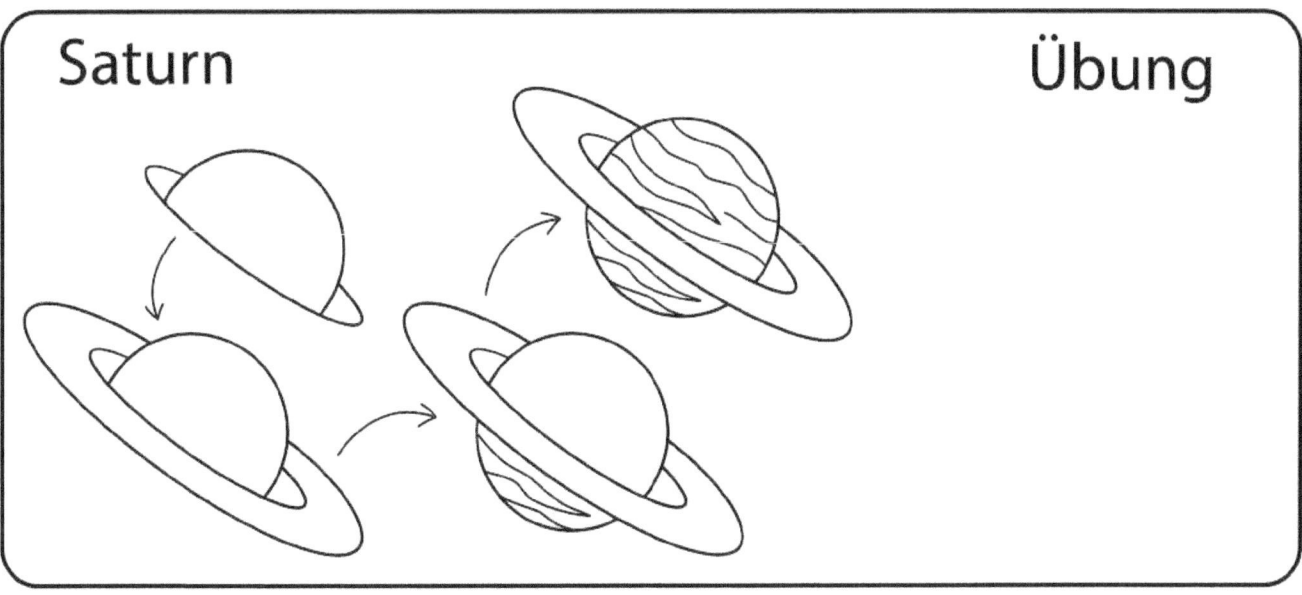

Rakete

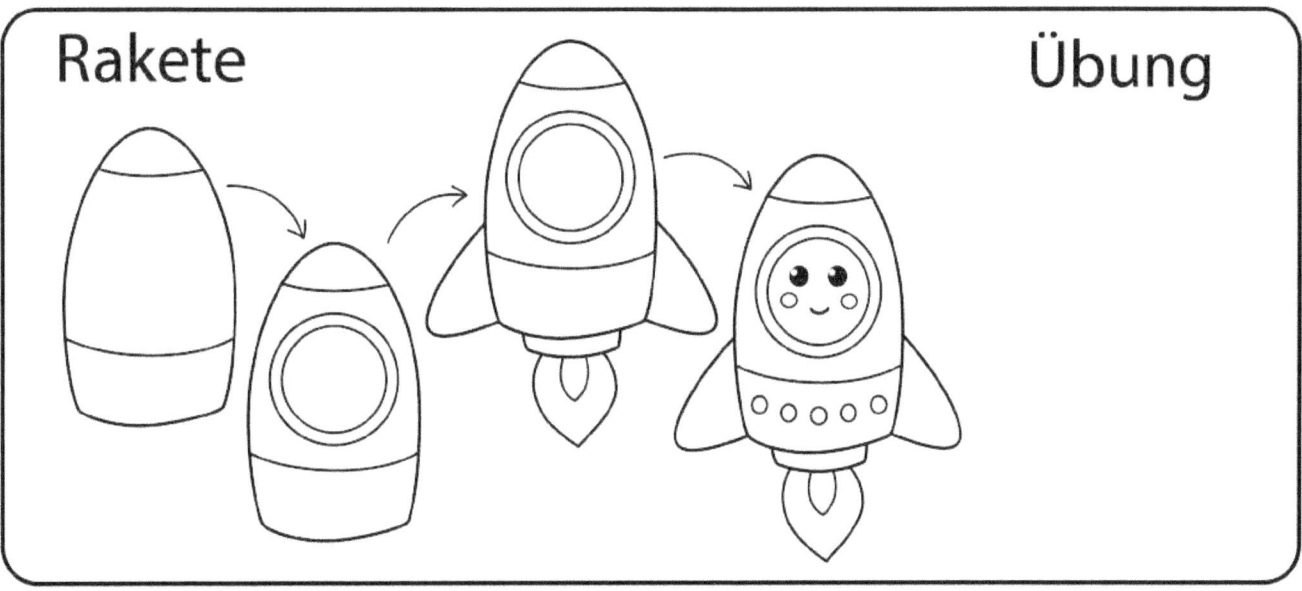

Lächelnde Sonne

Schlafender Mond

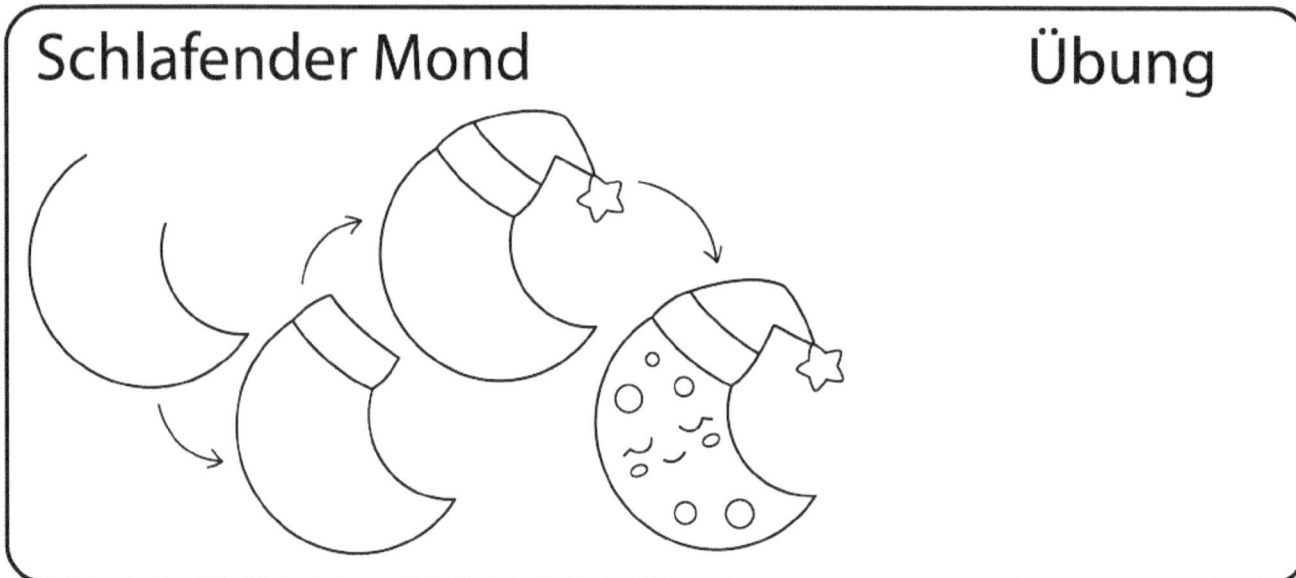

Sternschnuppe

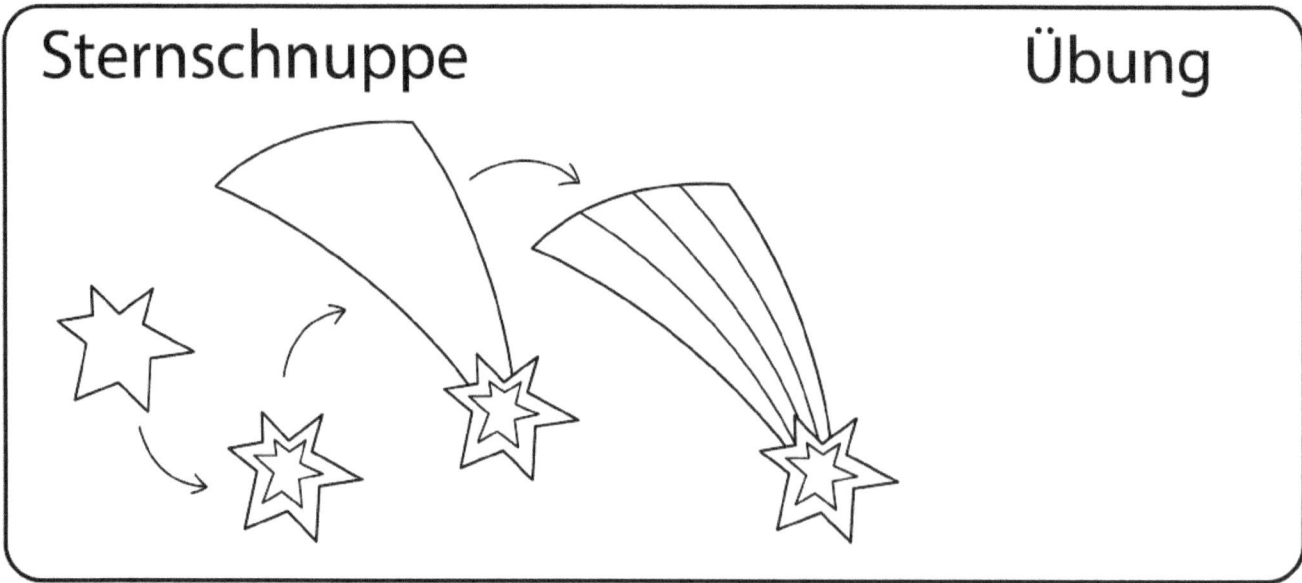

Phönix

Greif

Wasserspeier

Fee

Hexe

Zauberer

Einhorn Übung

Einhorn Übung

Kleines Pony Übung

Meerjungfrau Übung

Meerjungfrau Übung

Meermann Übung

Vampir Übung

Pirat Übung

Vampirfledermaus Übung

Wolf

Geist

Spinnennetz

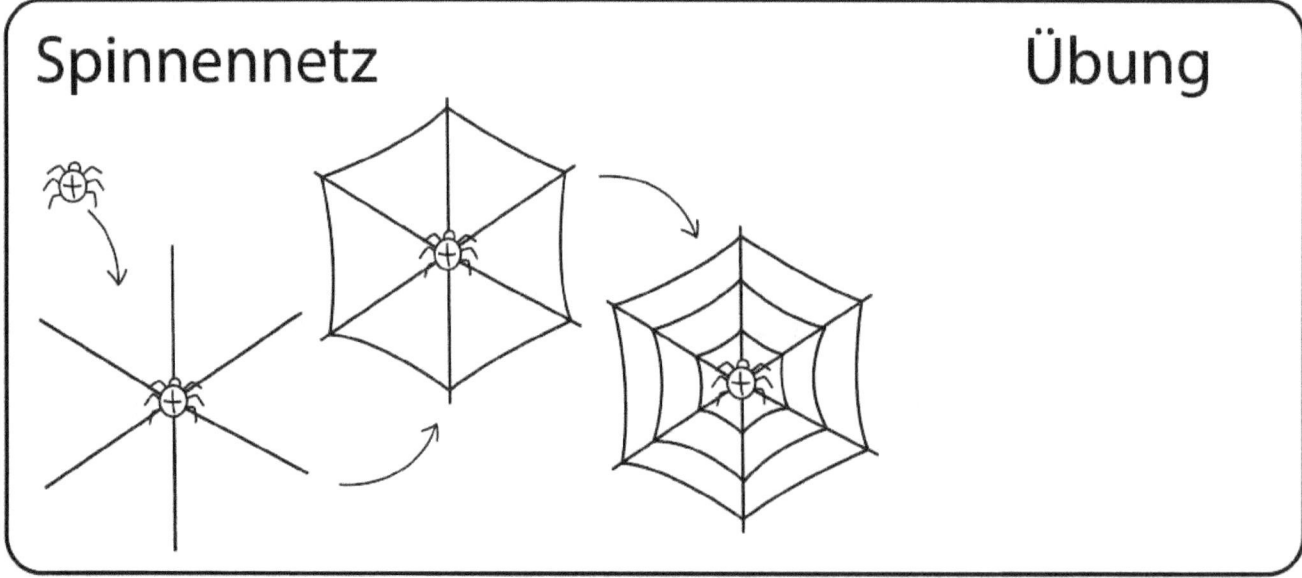

Skelett

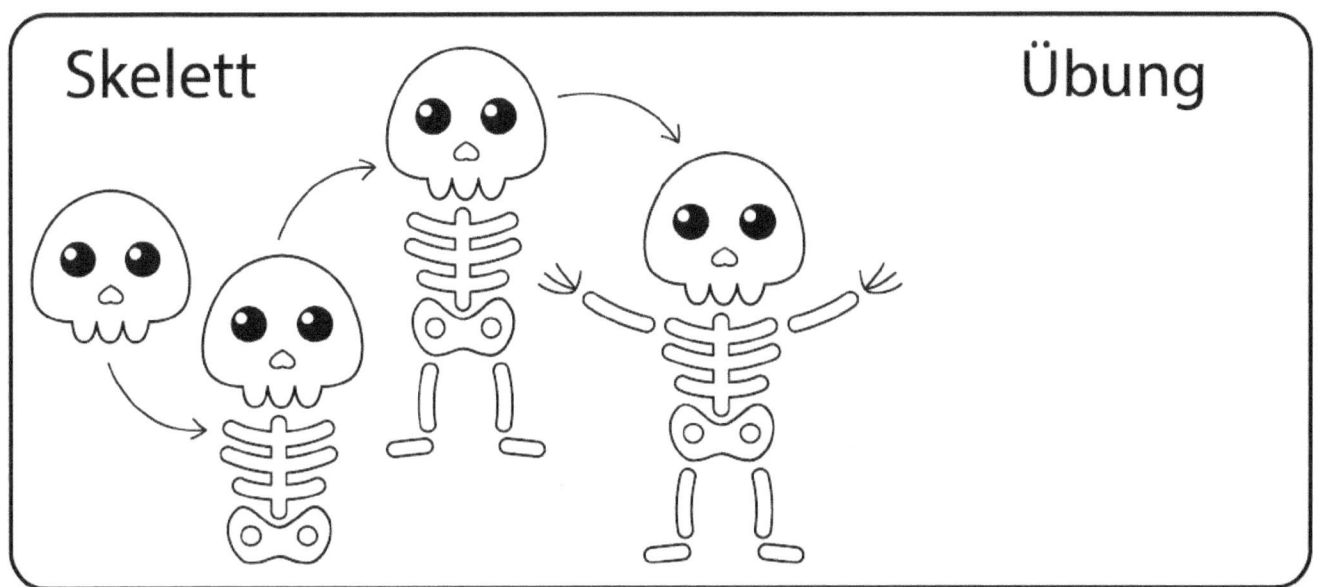

Schädel

Monsterauge

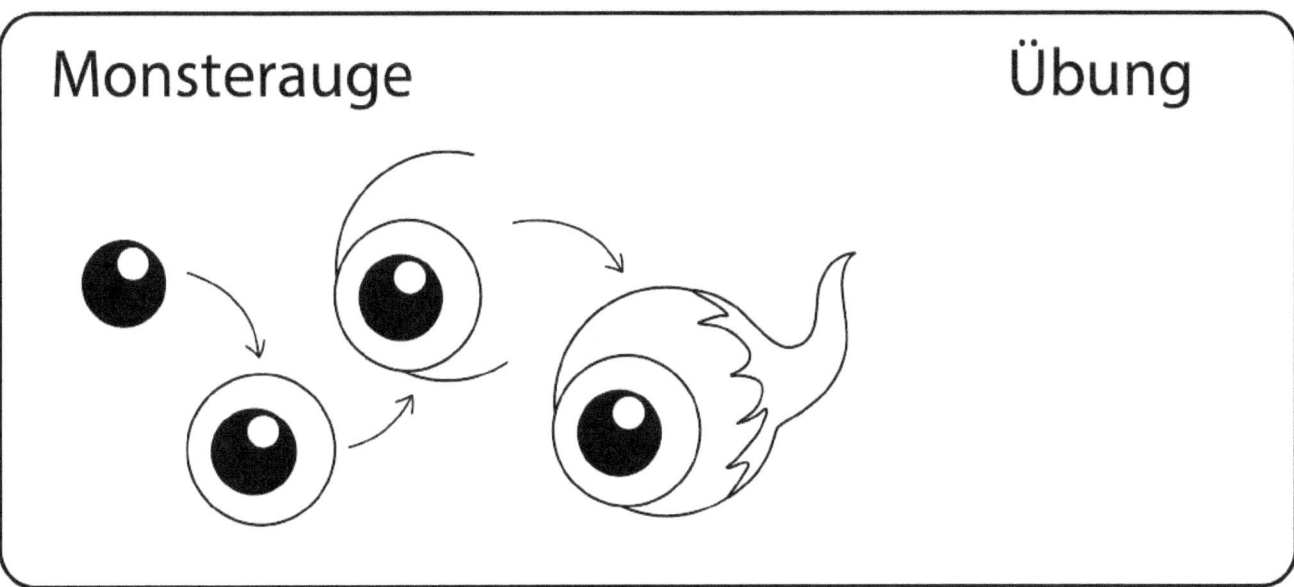

Mumie

Mumien-Katze

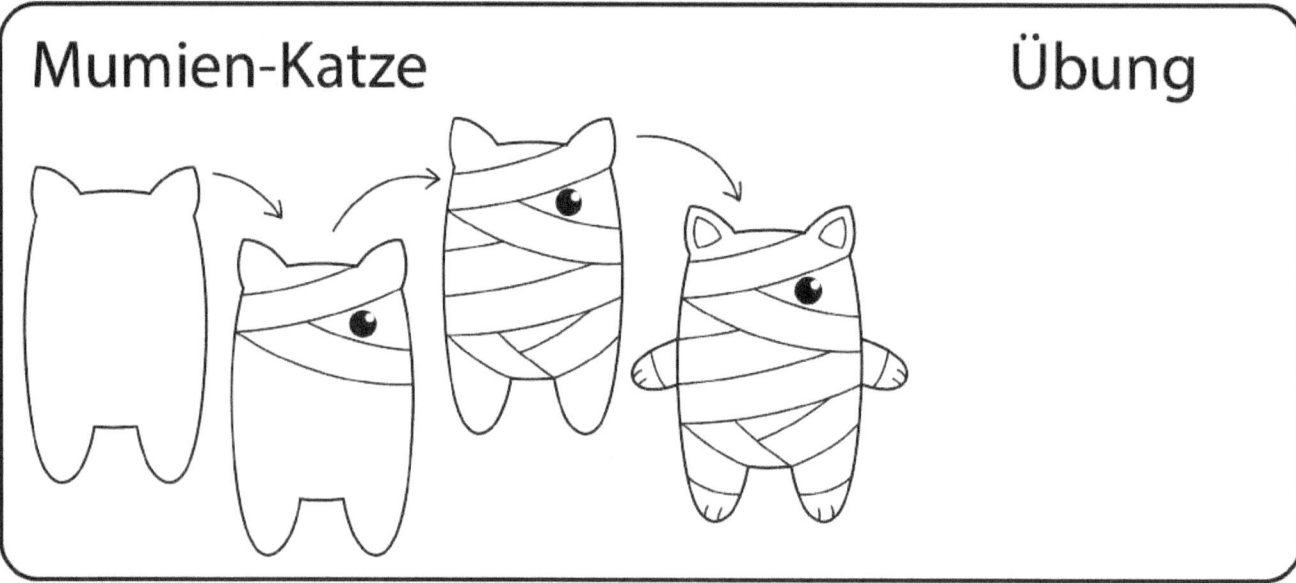

Zombie

Kürbislaterne

Kürbiskopf-Monster

Frankenstein-Monster

Teleskop Übung

Der Mars Übung

Mars-Rover Übung

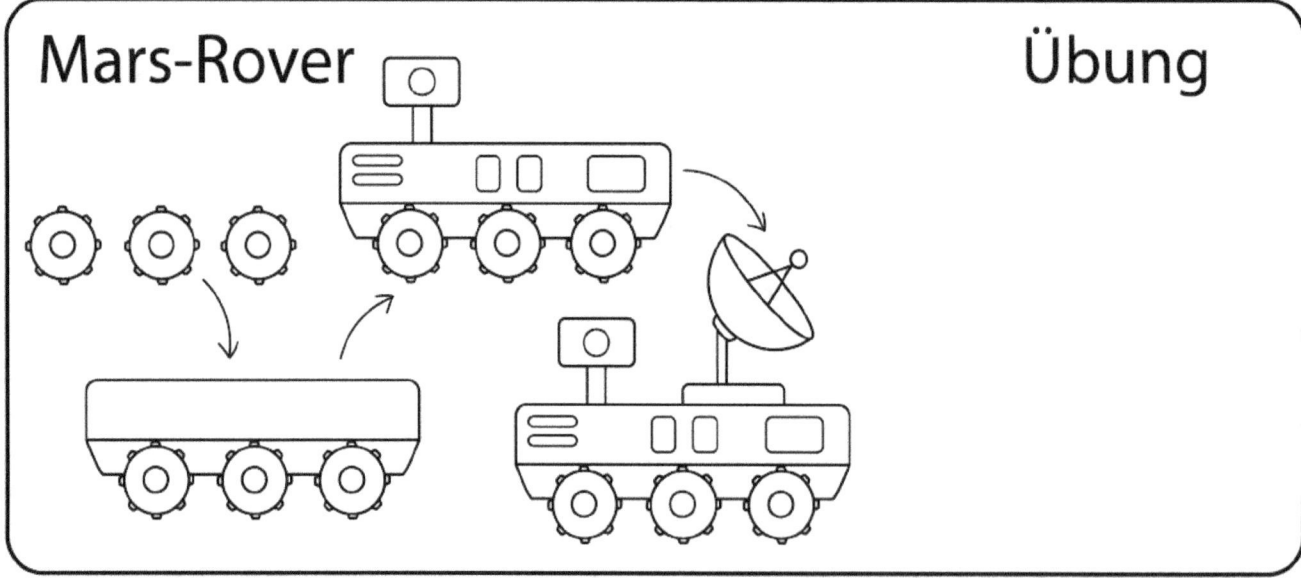

Rentier

Pinguin

Katze in Socke

Rentier

Weihnachtsbär

Weihnachtskatze

Weihnachtsglocken Übung

Weihnachtskranz Übung

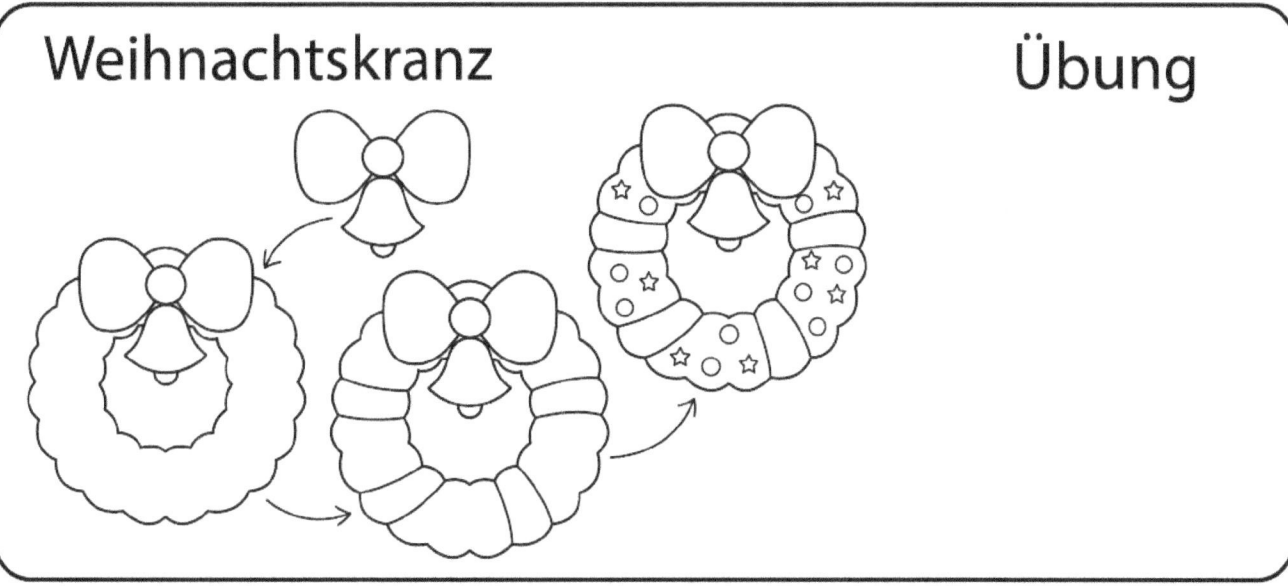

Weihnachtsgeschenk Übung

Weihnachtsmann Übung

Frau Weihnachtsmann Übung

Weihnachtsbaum Übung

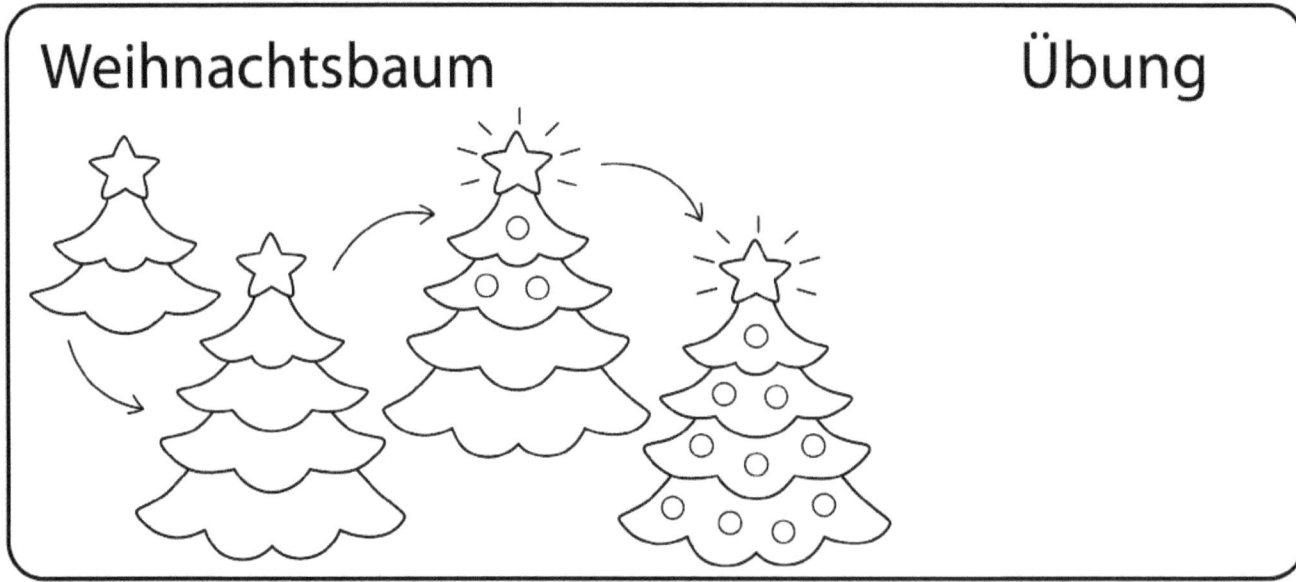

Drache Übung

Drache Übung

Drachenbaby Übung

Tyrannosaurus Rex Baby Übung

Triceratops Baby Übung

Brontosaurus im Ei Übung

Iguanodon

Spinosaurus

Pterodactylus im Ei

Plesiosaurus

Triceratops

Stegosaurus

Brachiosaurus Übung

Ouranosaurus Übung

Brontosaurus Übung

Narwal Übung

Tintenfisch Übung

Seepferdchen Übung

Niedliches Eis am Stiel

Niedlicher Lutscher

Niedlicher Cupcake

Niedliche Birne

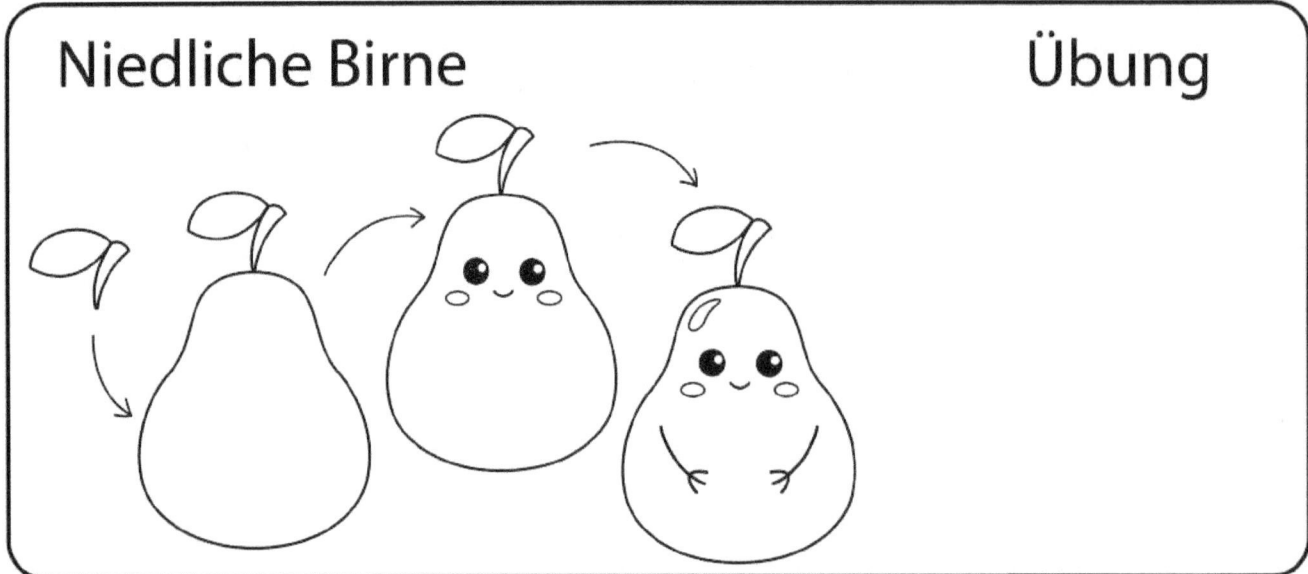

Niedlicher Apfel

Niedliche Avocado

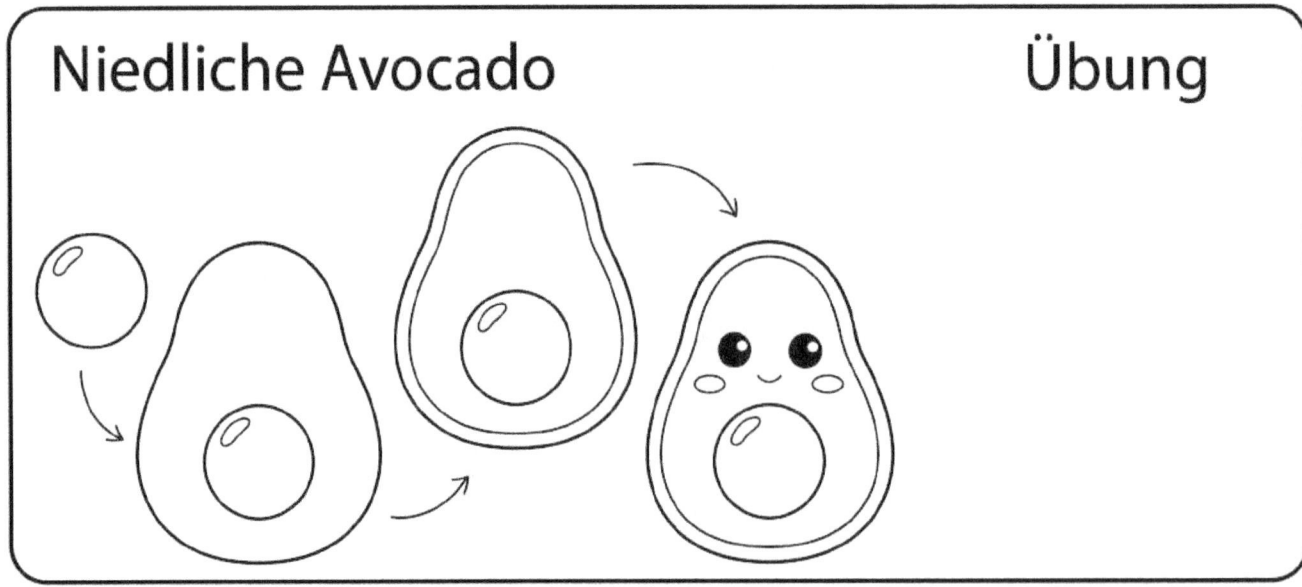

Niedlicher Kaffee Übung

Niedliche Tassenkatze Übung

Niedlicher Tassenhund Übung

Niedlicher Kaffeehase Übung

Niedliches Kaffeekaninchen Übung

Niedliche Eistüte Übung

Niedlicher Donut Übung

Niedlicher Einhorn-Donut Übung

Niedlicher Panda-Donut Übung

Lebkuchenmann Übung

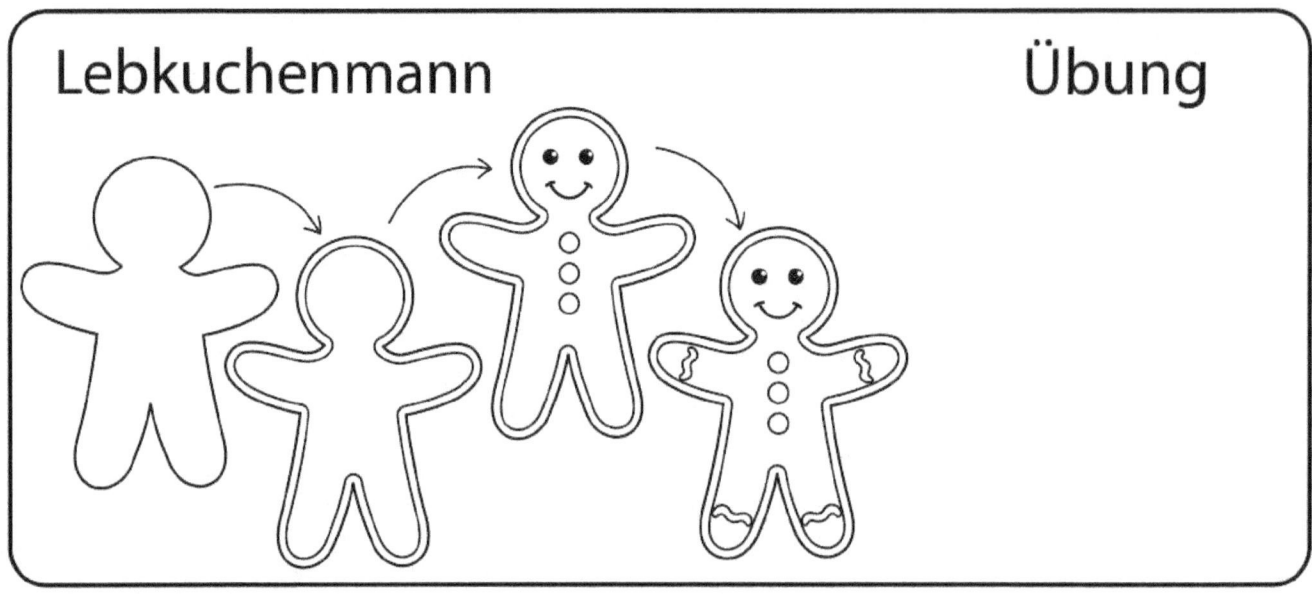

Lutscher Übung

Zuckerstange Übung

Hut

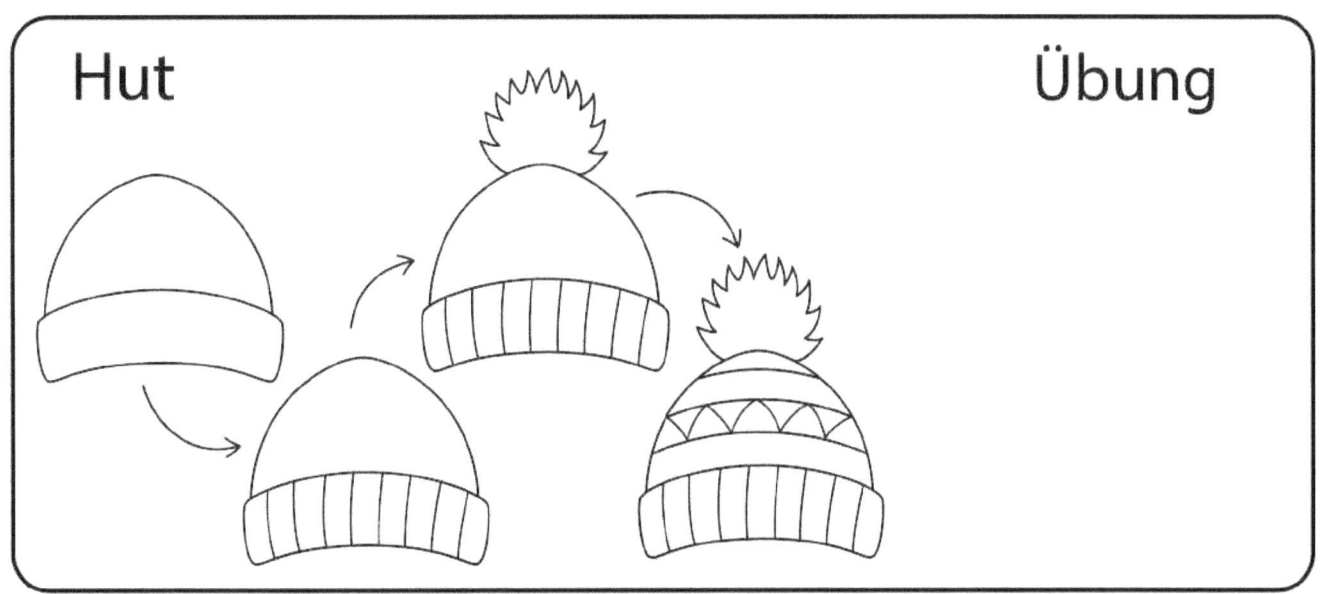

Schal

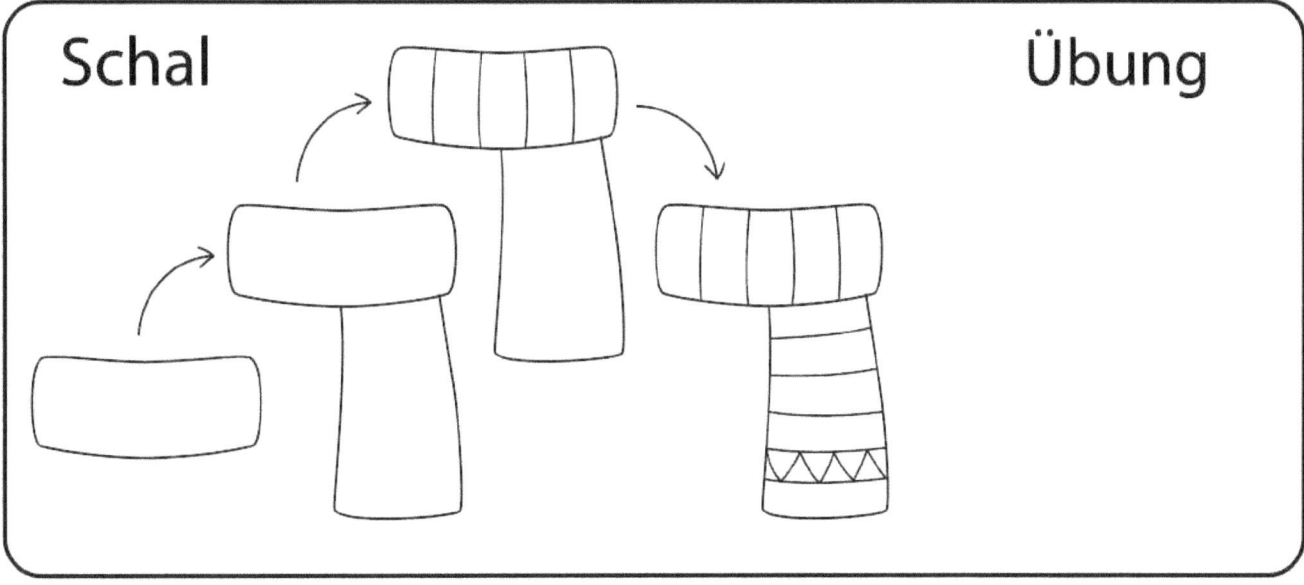

Handschuhe

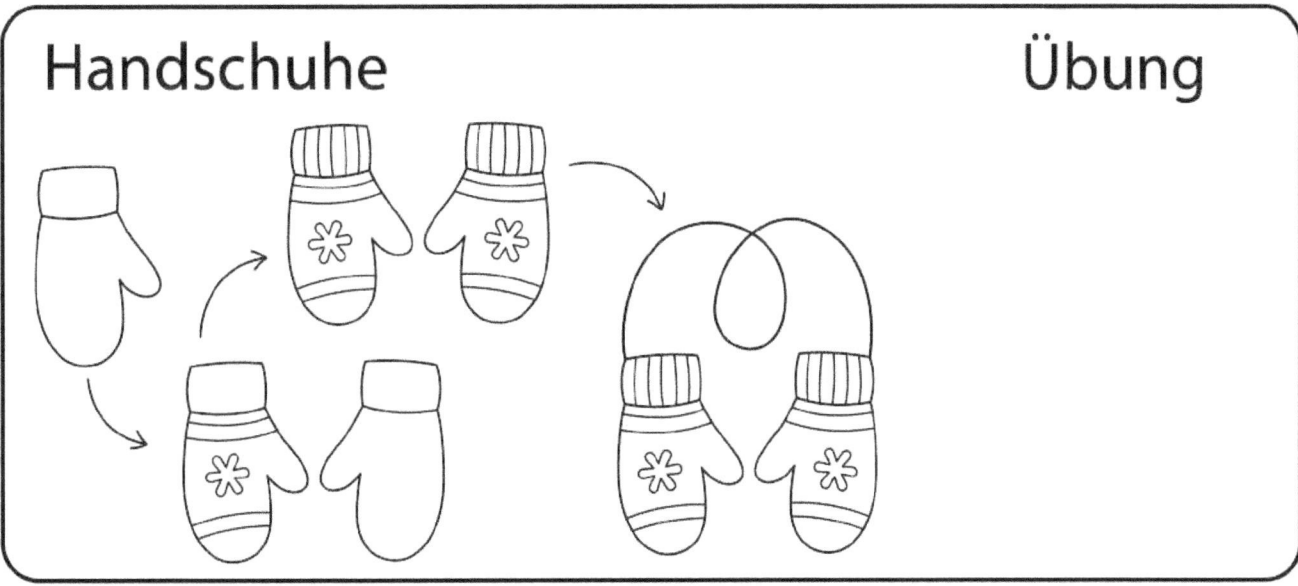

Engel

Elf

Schlitten des Weihnachtsmanns

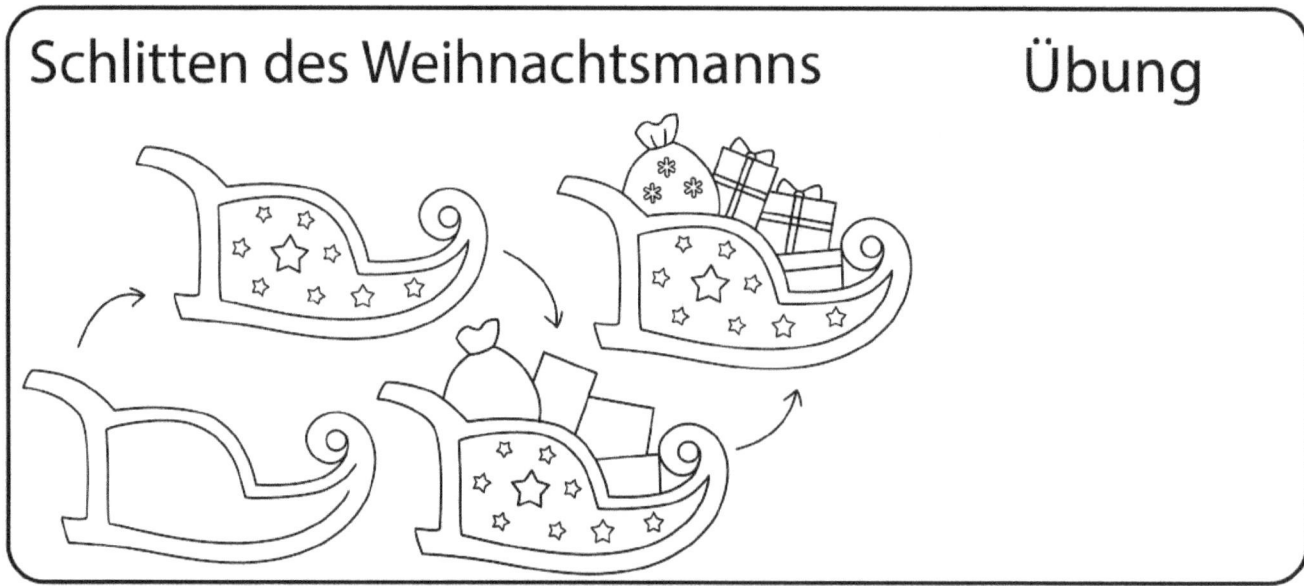

Schneemann Übung

Schneeflocke Übung

Schlitten Übung

Weihnachtsstrumpf Übung

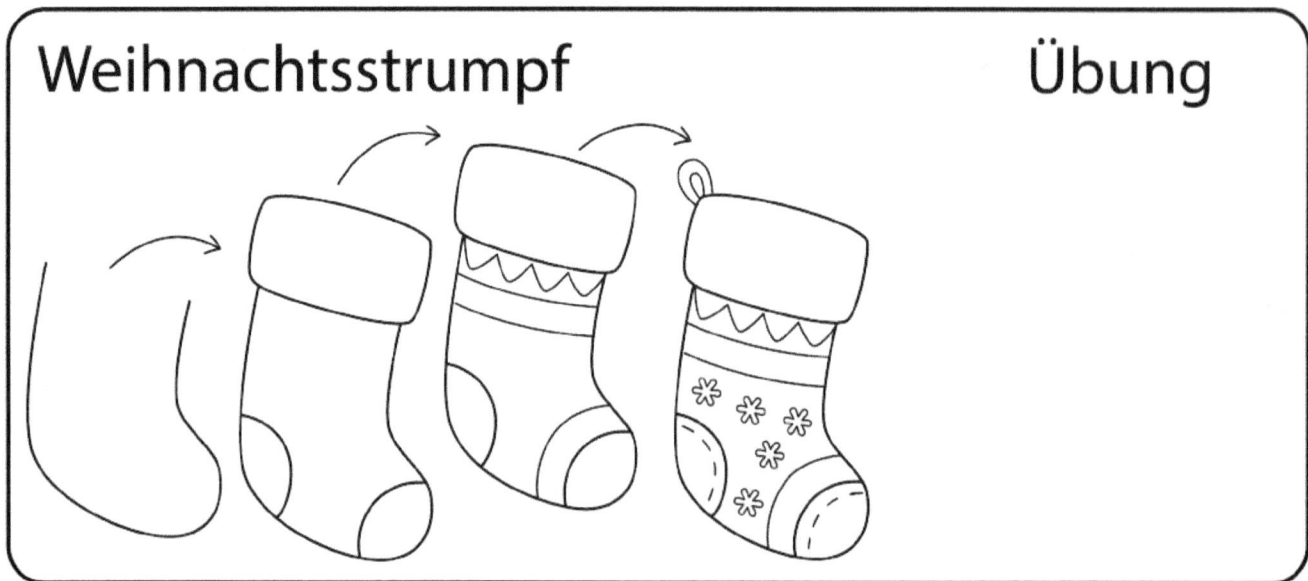

Weihnachtsbaumkugel Übung

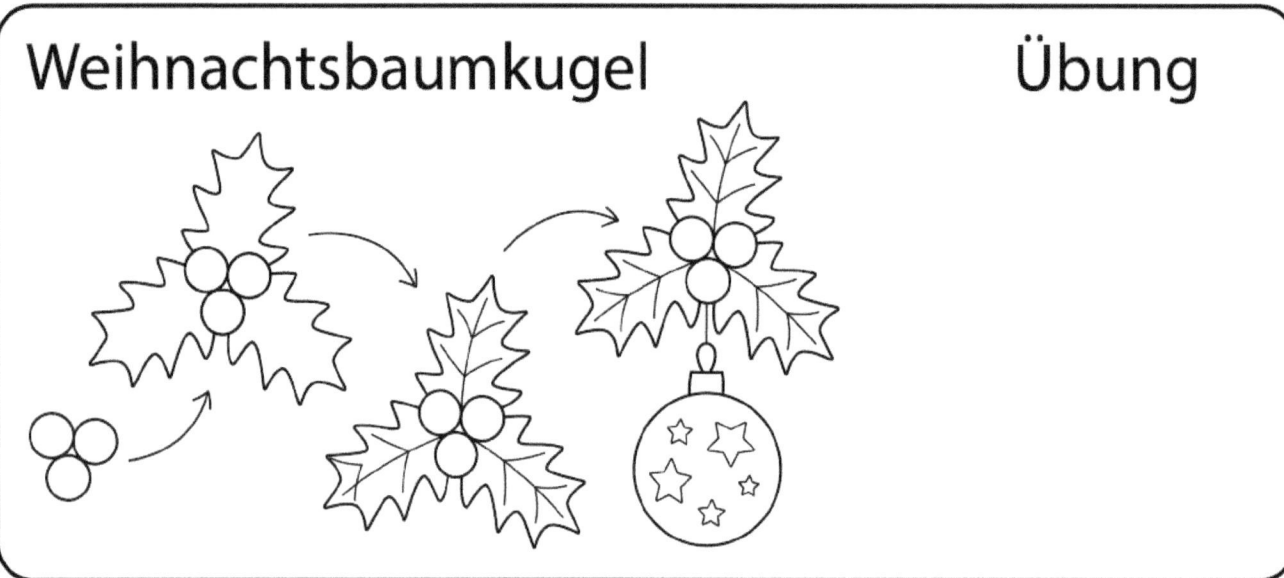

Lebkuchenmann Übung

Wigwam Übung

Iglu Übung

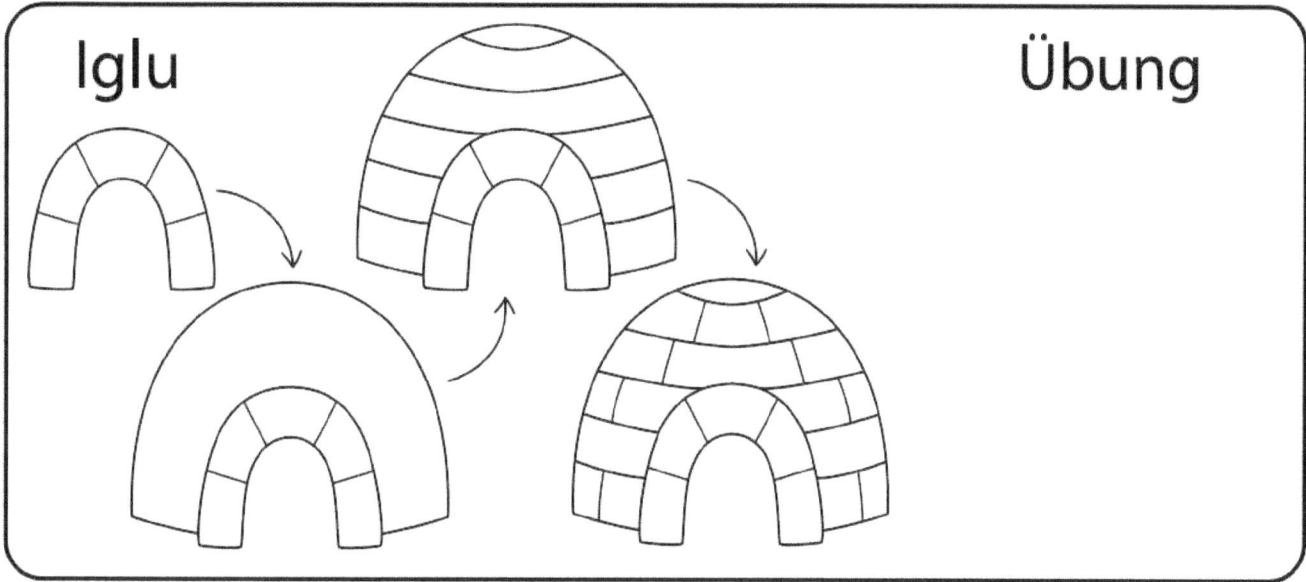

Leuchtturm Übung

Haus

Schloss

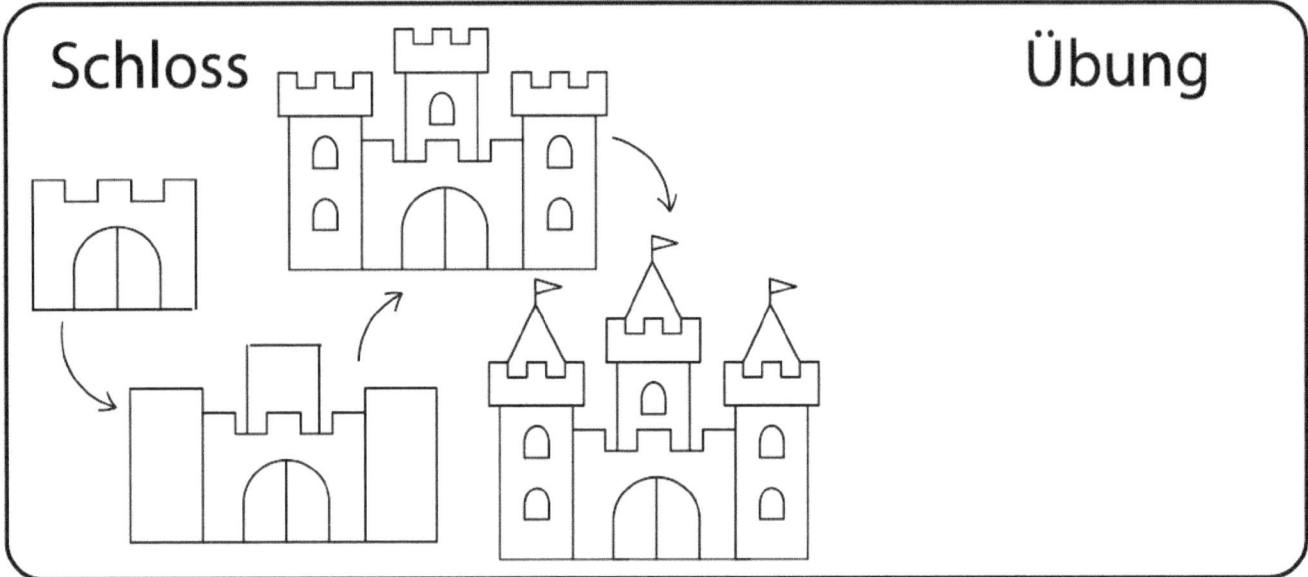

Windmühle

Niedliche Prinzessin Übung

Niedlicher Prinz Übung

Niedliches Einhorn Übung

Niedlicher Dinosaurier Übung

Niedlicher Dinosaurier Übung

Niedlicher Dinosaurier Übung

Niedliche Regenwolke

Niedliche Einhornkatze

Niedlicher Tassenfaultier

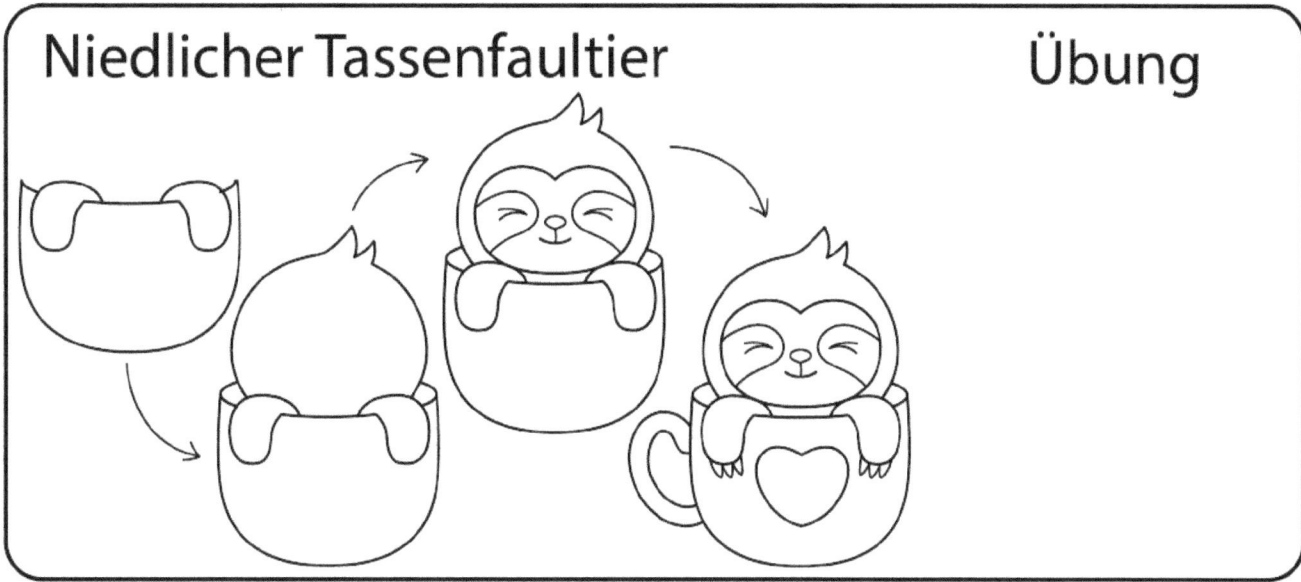

Niedliche Ananas

Niedliche Banane

Niedlicher Pilz

Niedlicher Keks Übung

Niedliche Milch Übung

Niedliche Macarons Übung

Niedliche Pommes Übung

Niedlicher Hotdog Übung

Niedlicher Taco Übung

Niedlicher Toast

Niedlicher Speck

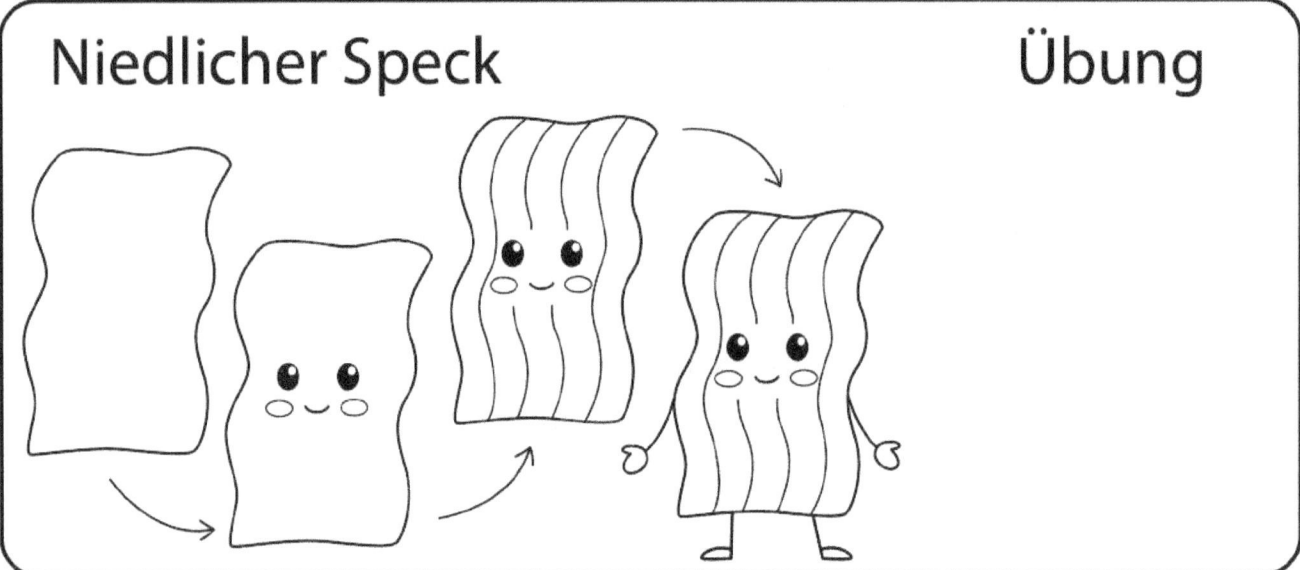

Niedliches Ei

Schulbus Übung

Straßenbahn Übung

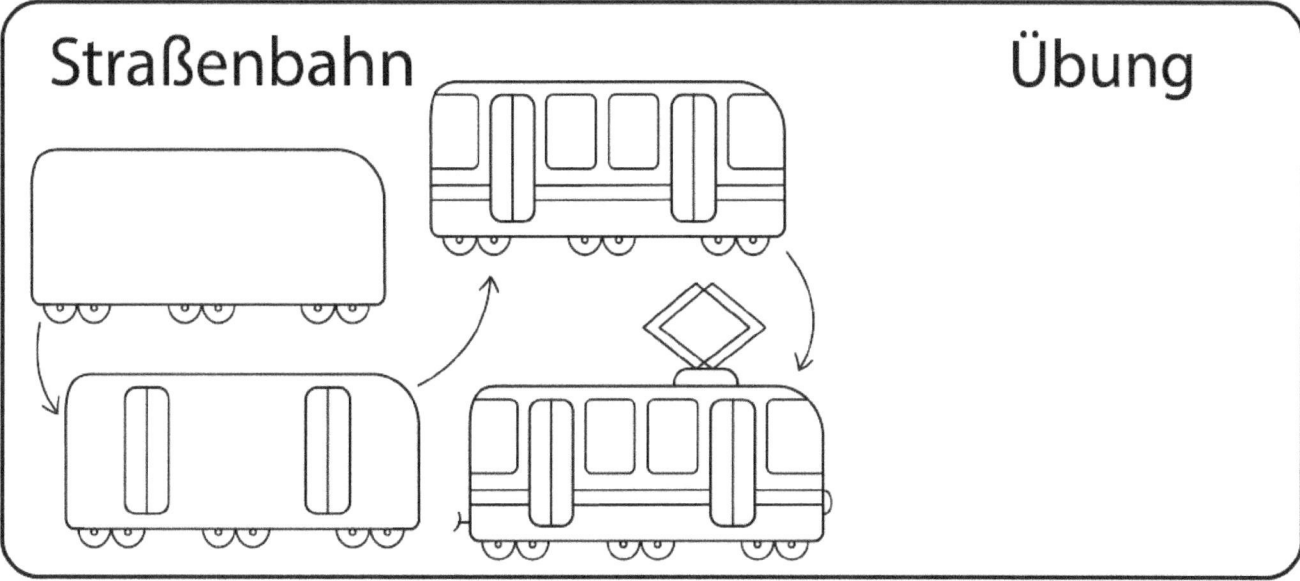

Zug Übung

Bagger Übung

Kran Übung

Walze Übung

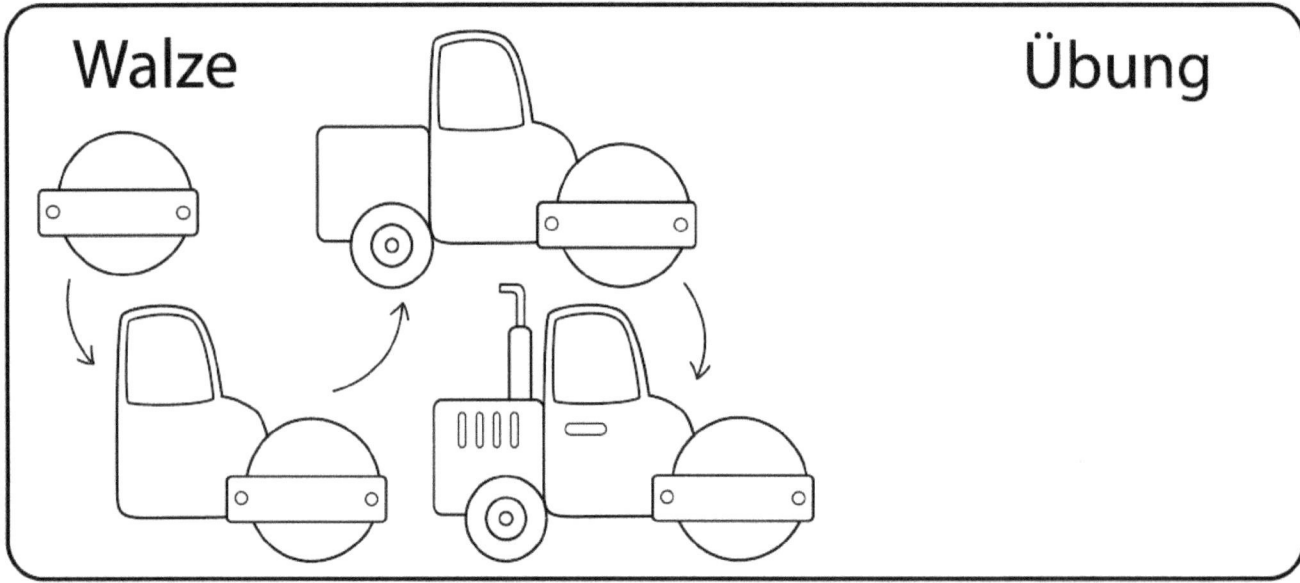

Feuerwehrauto Übung

Kipplaster Übung

Tanklaster Übung

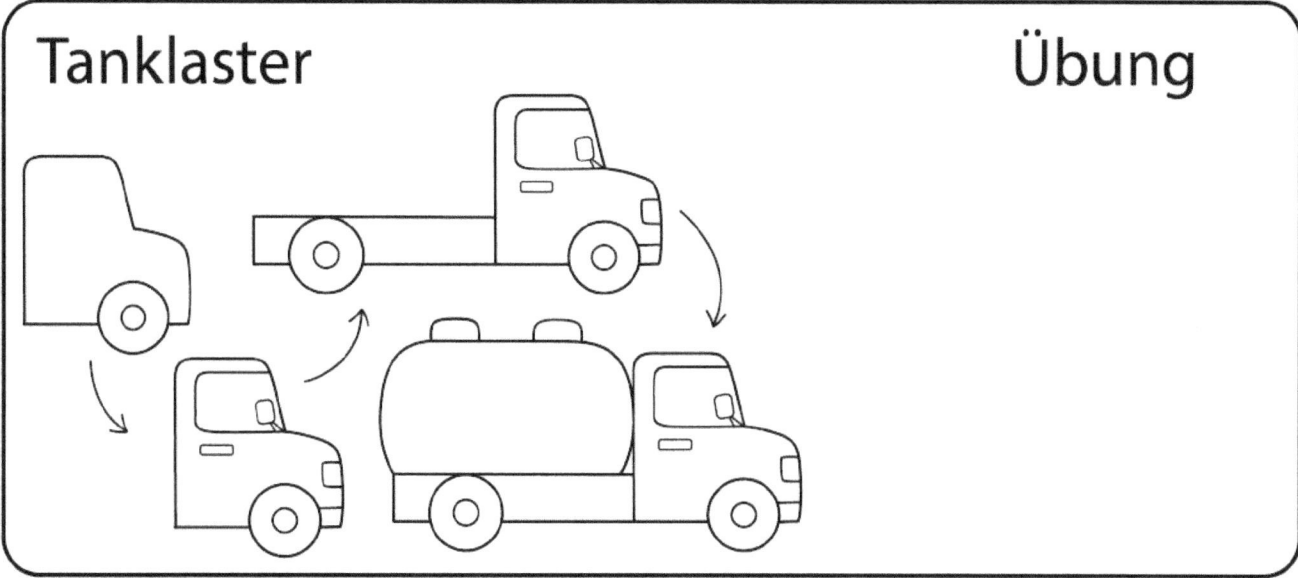

Fahrrad Übung

Motorrad Übung

Motorrad Übung

Segelboot Übung

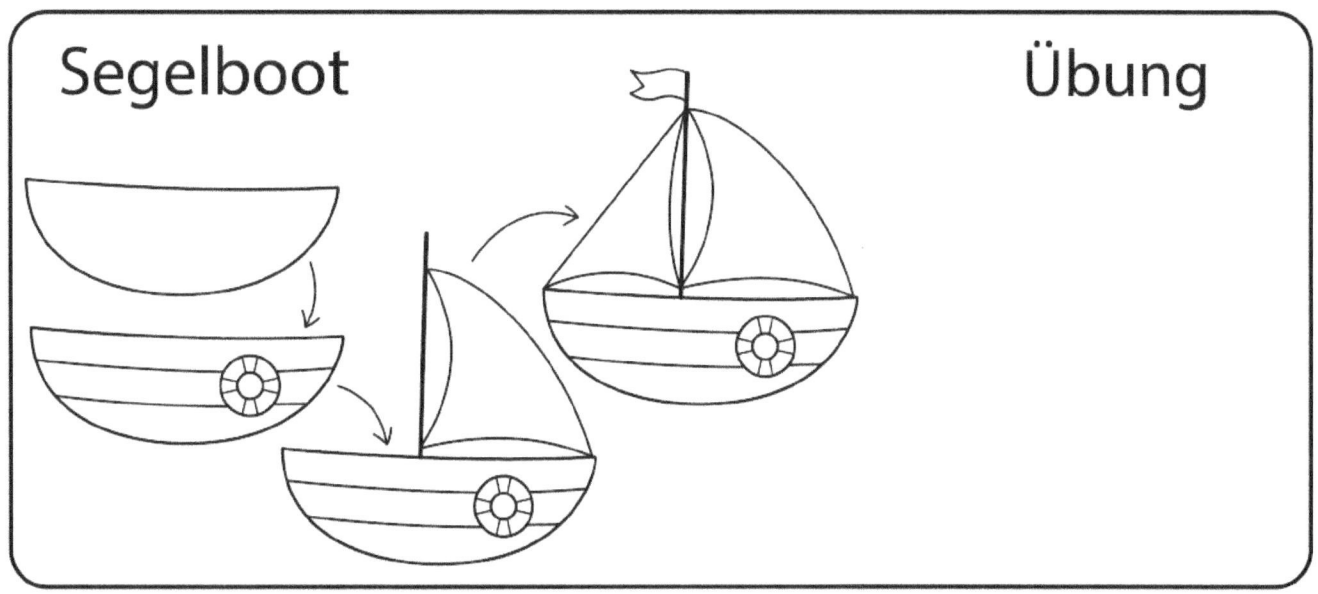

Schlepper Übung

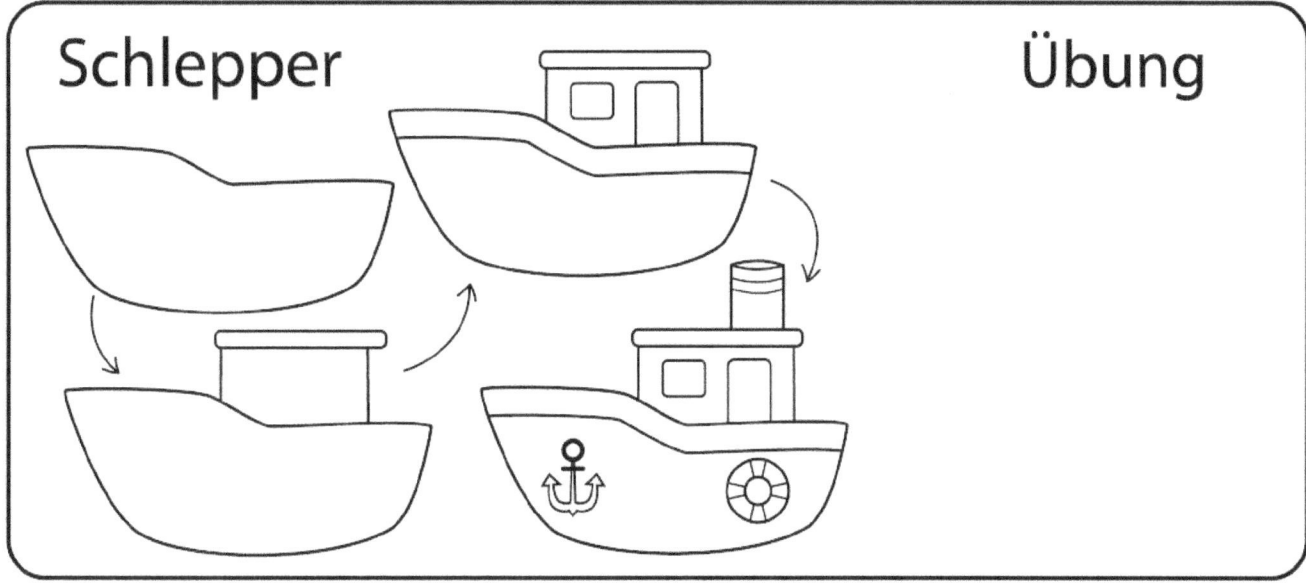

U-Boot Übung

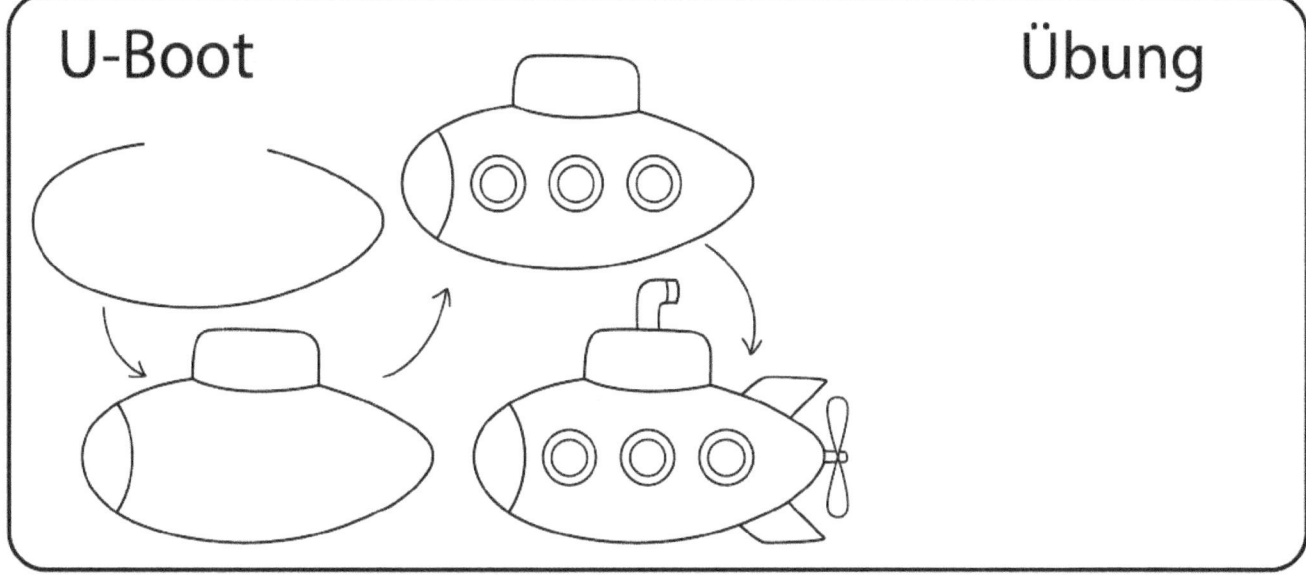

Jet-Ski

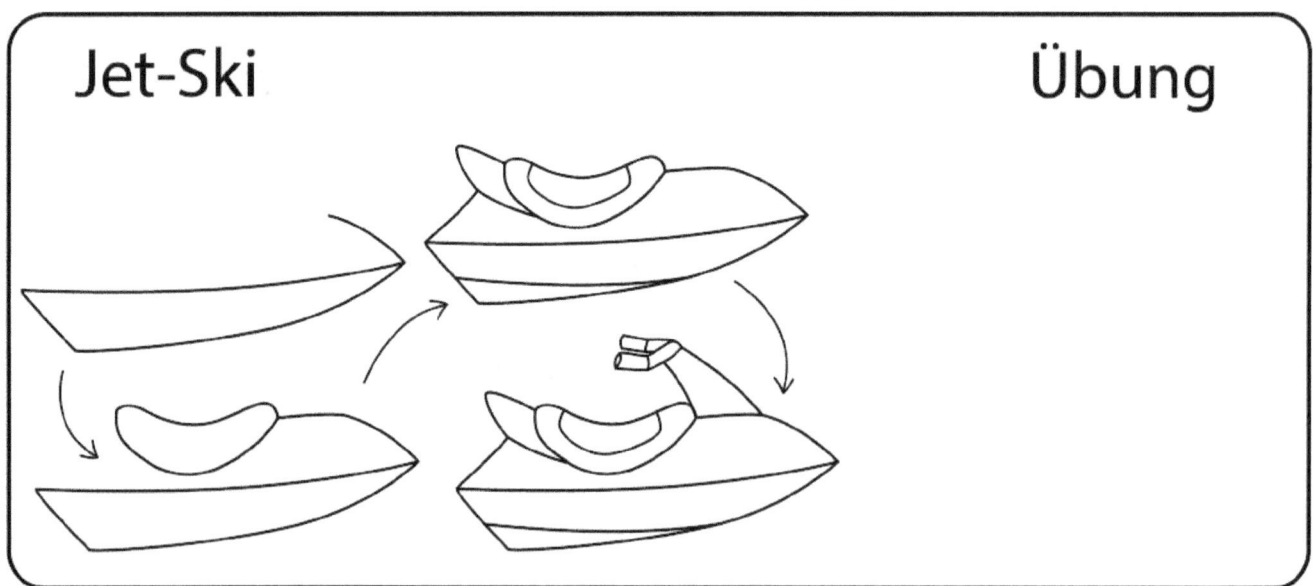

U-Boot

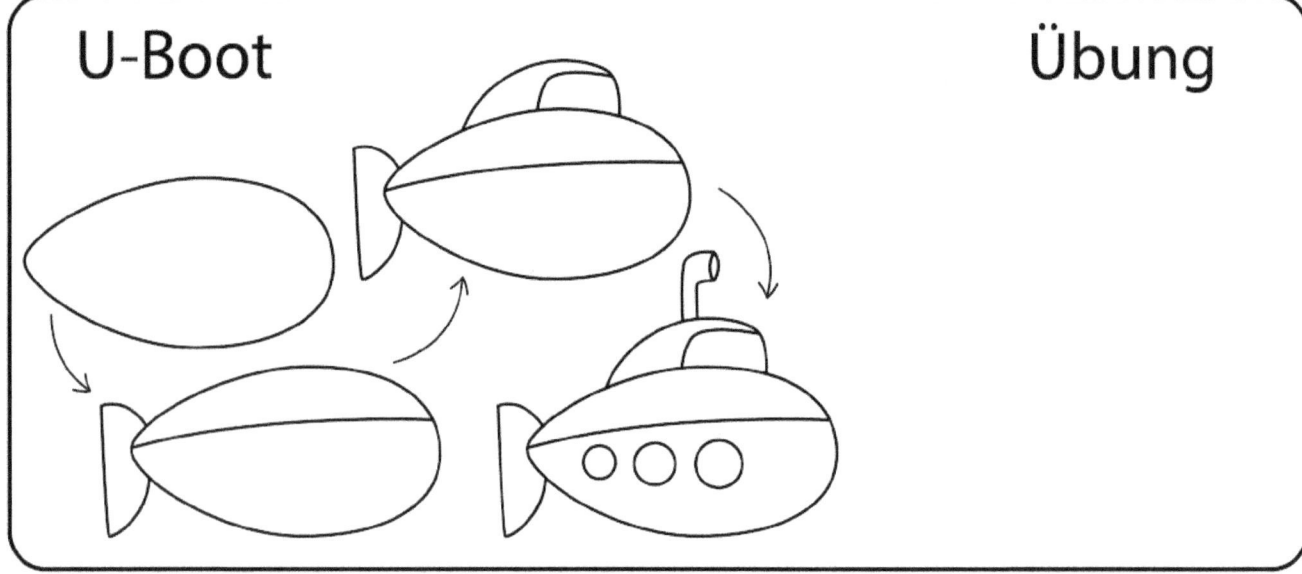

Luftschiff

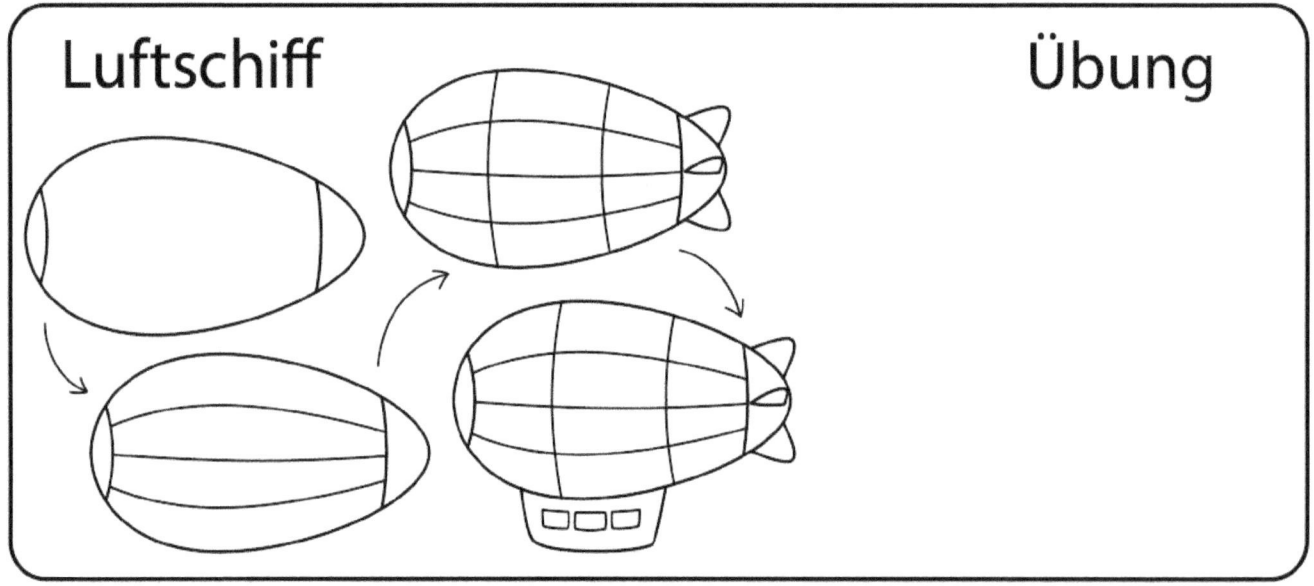

Abschleppwagen Übung

Gabelstapler Übung

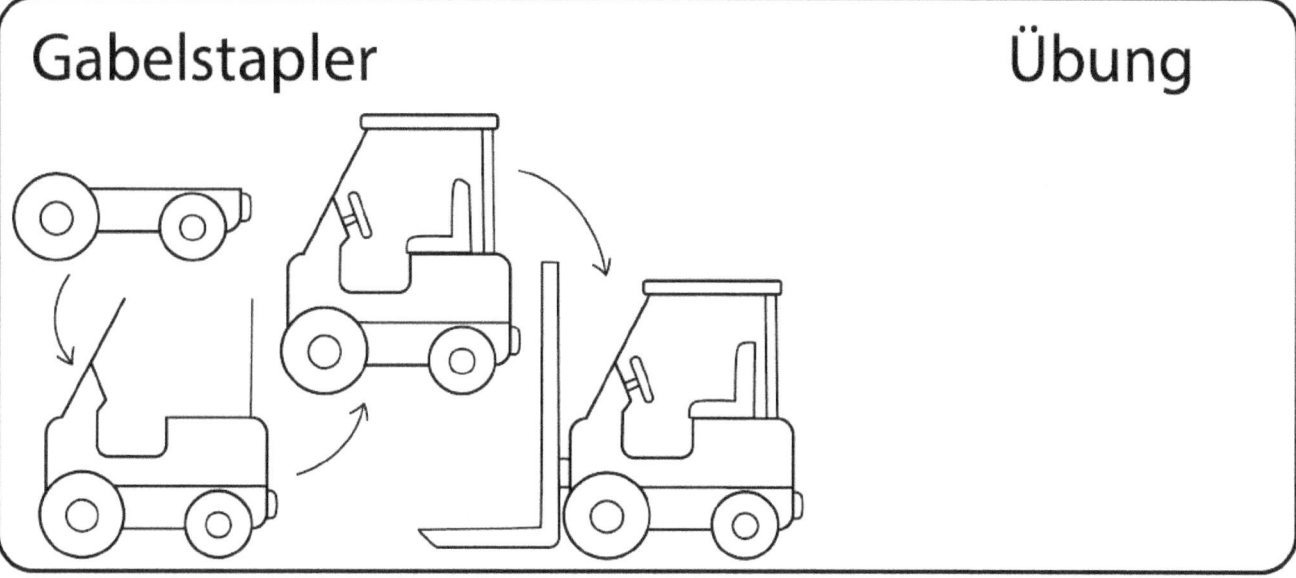

Zementmischer Übung

Flugzeug

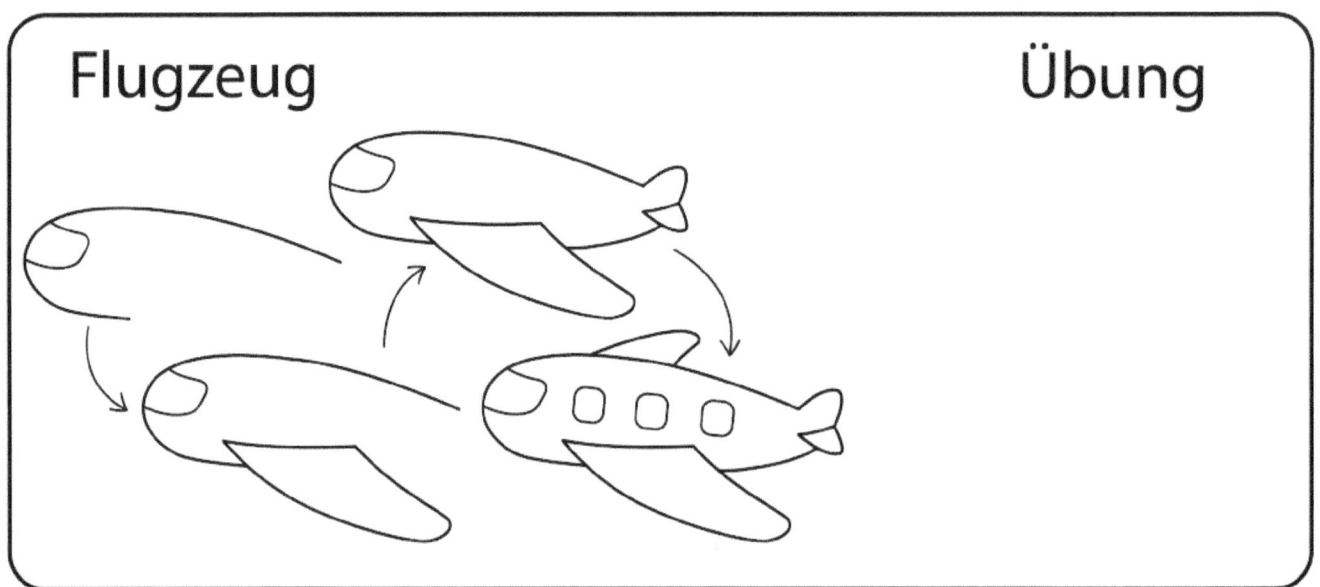

Hubschrauber

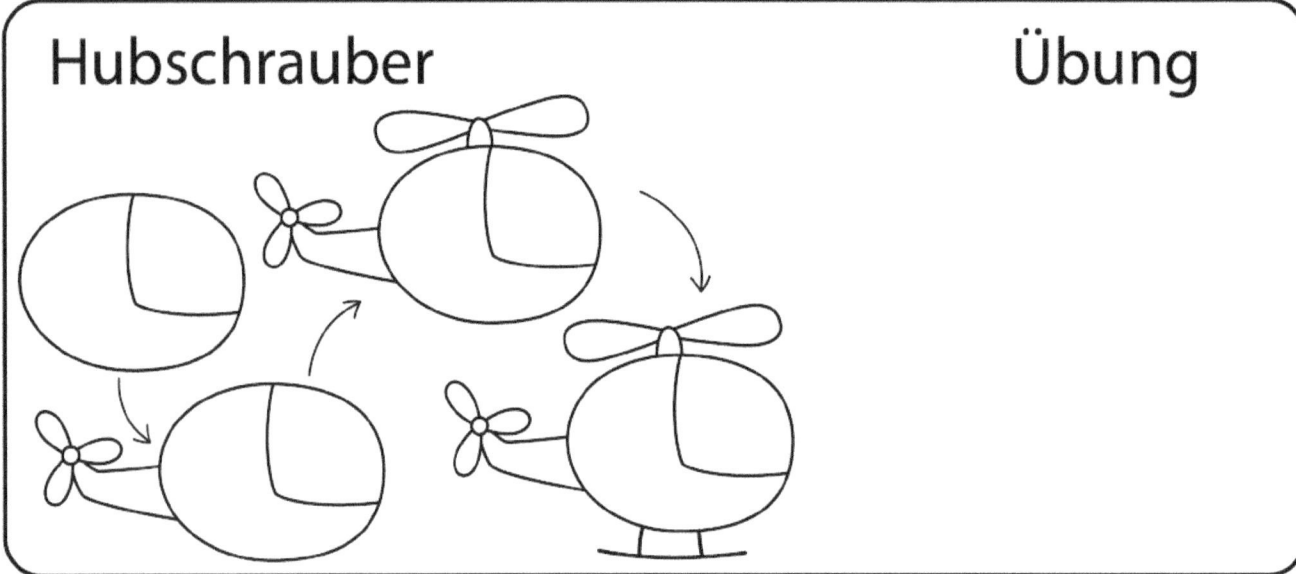

Heißluftballon

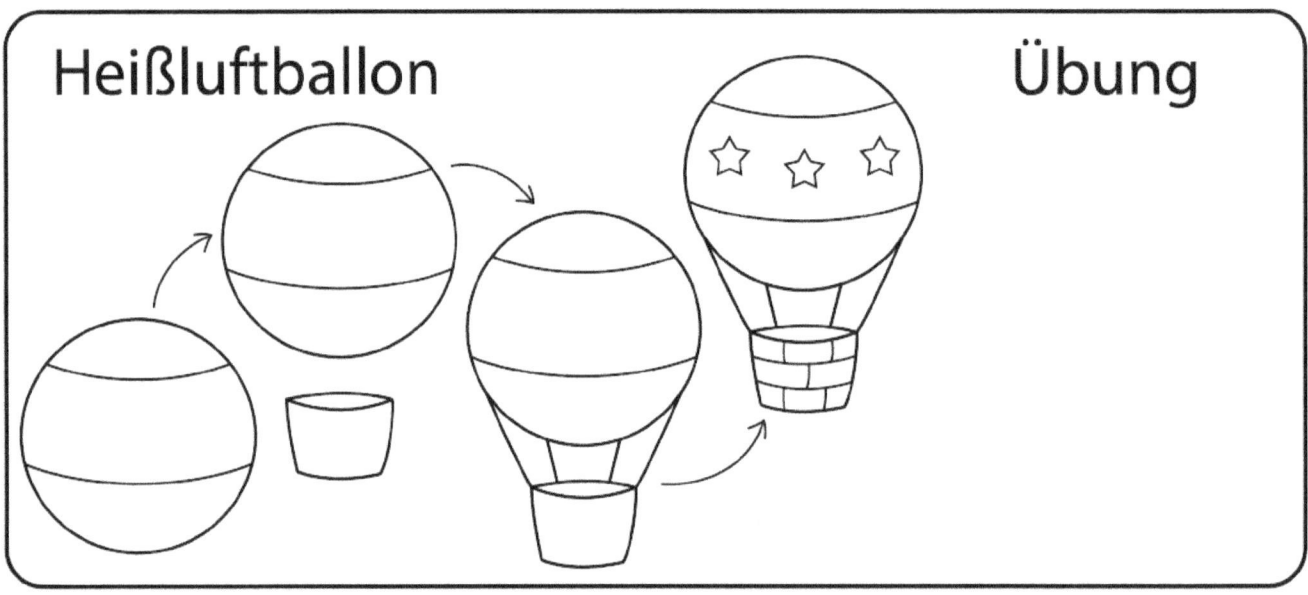

Taxi

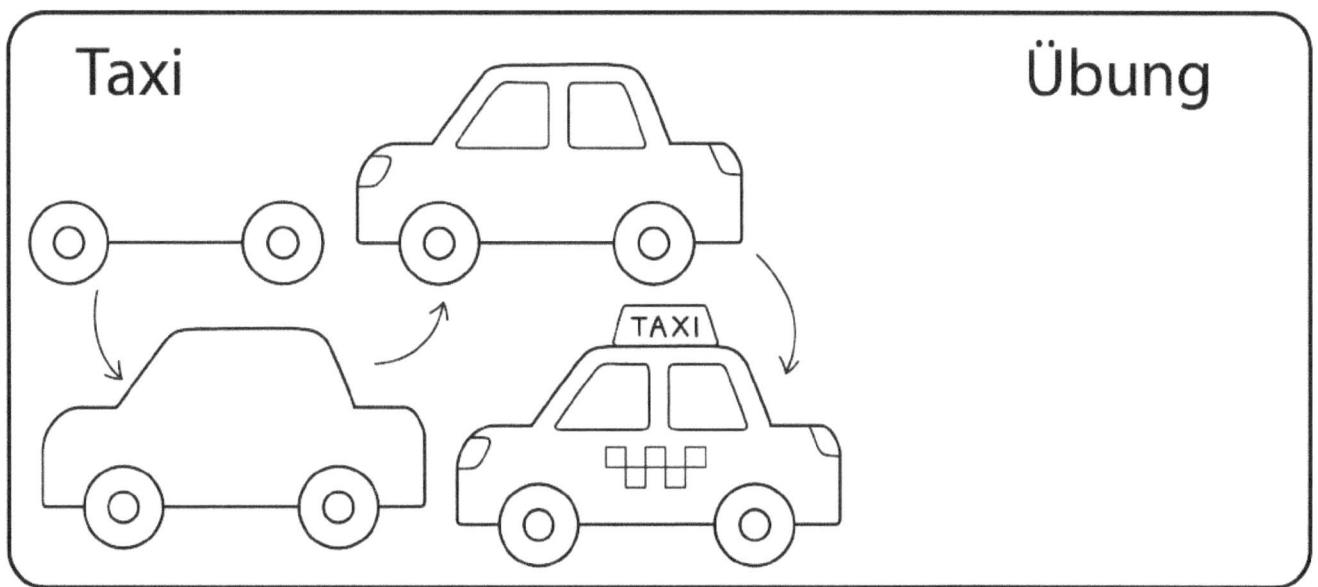

Traktor

Kipplaster

Polizeiauto Übung

Krankenwagen Übung

Auto Übung

Globus Übung

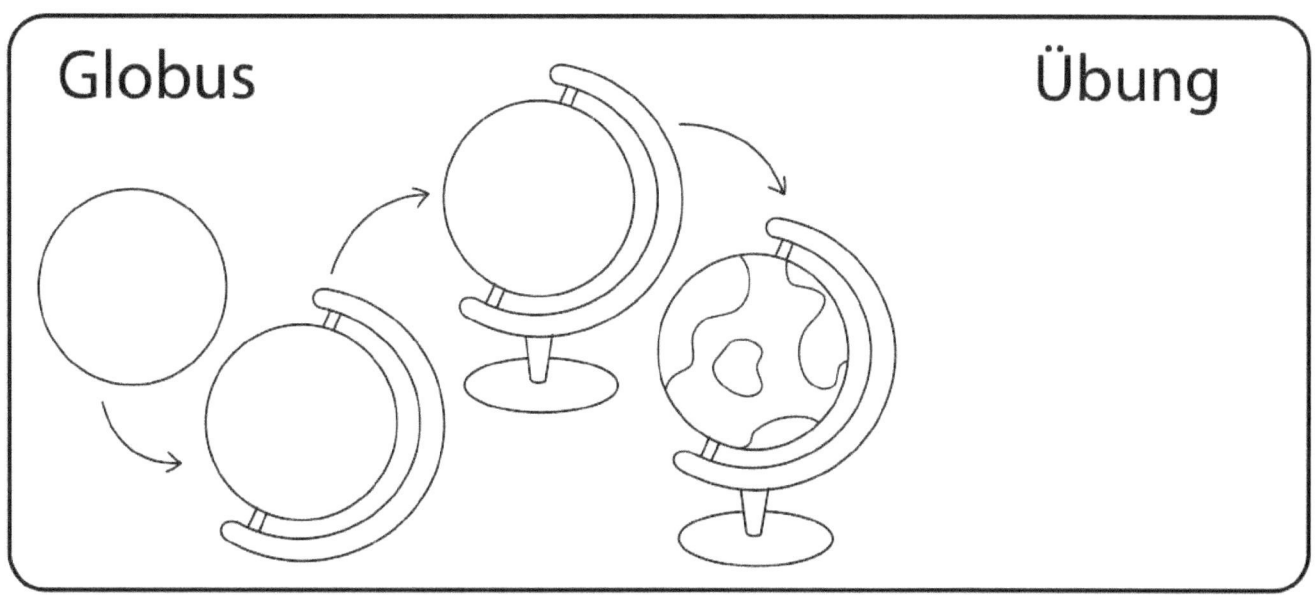

Lupe Übung

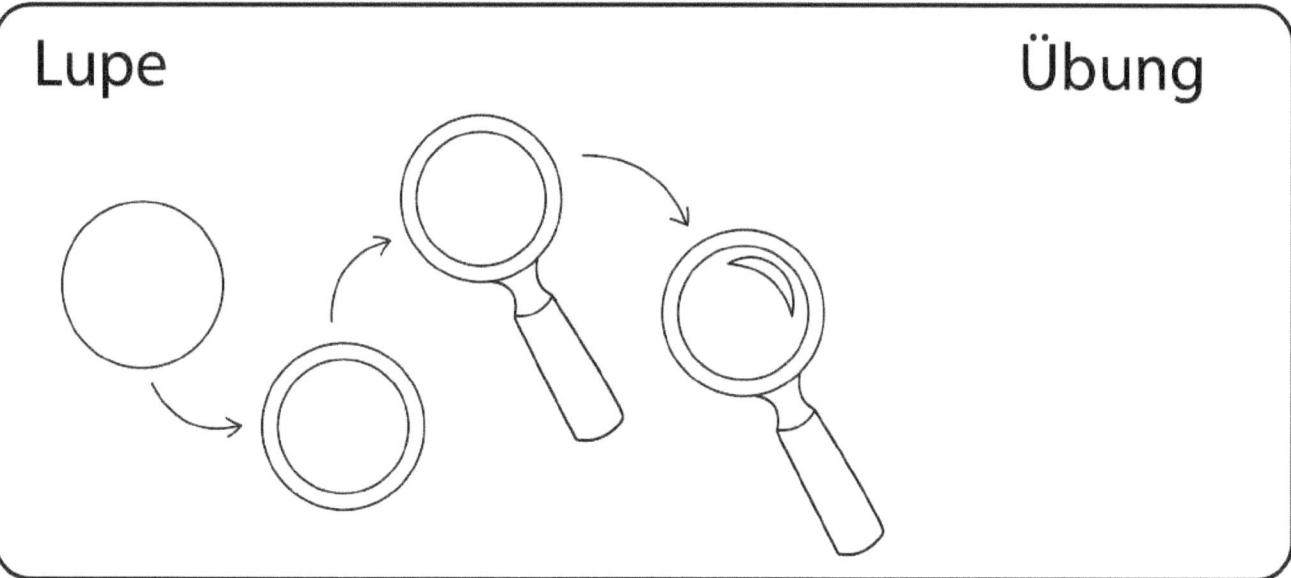

Reagenzgläser Übung

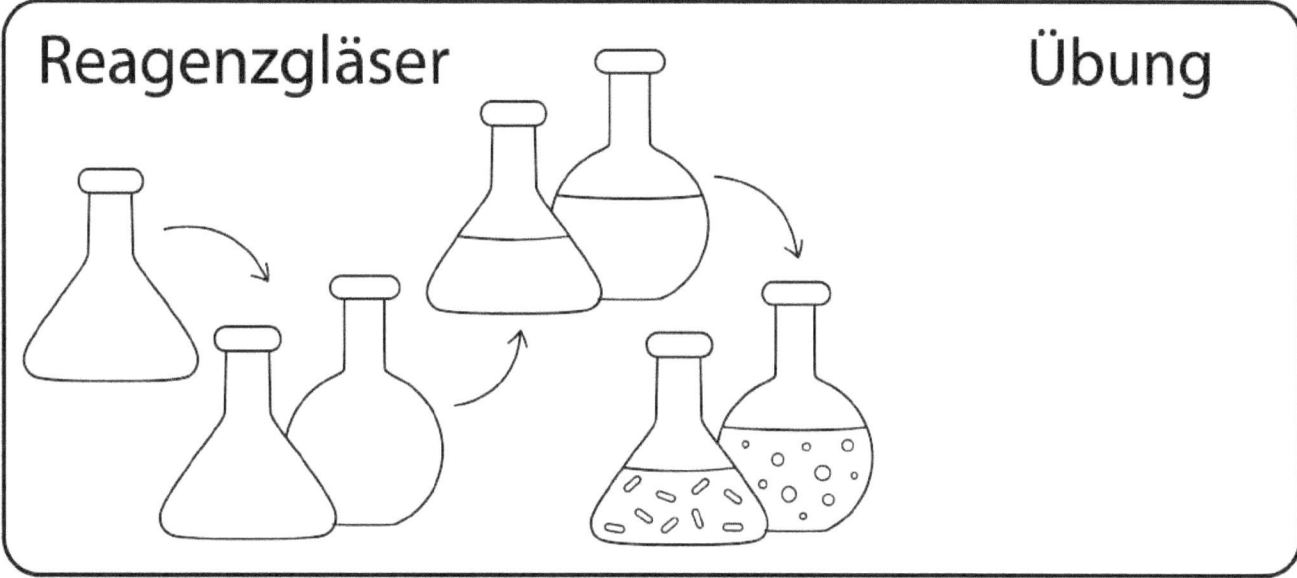

Federmäppchen

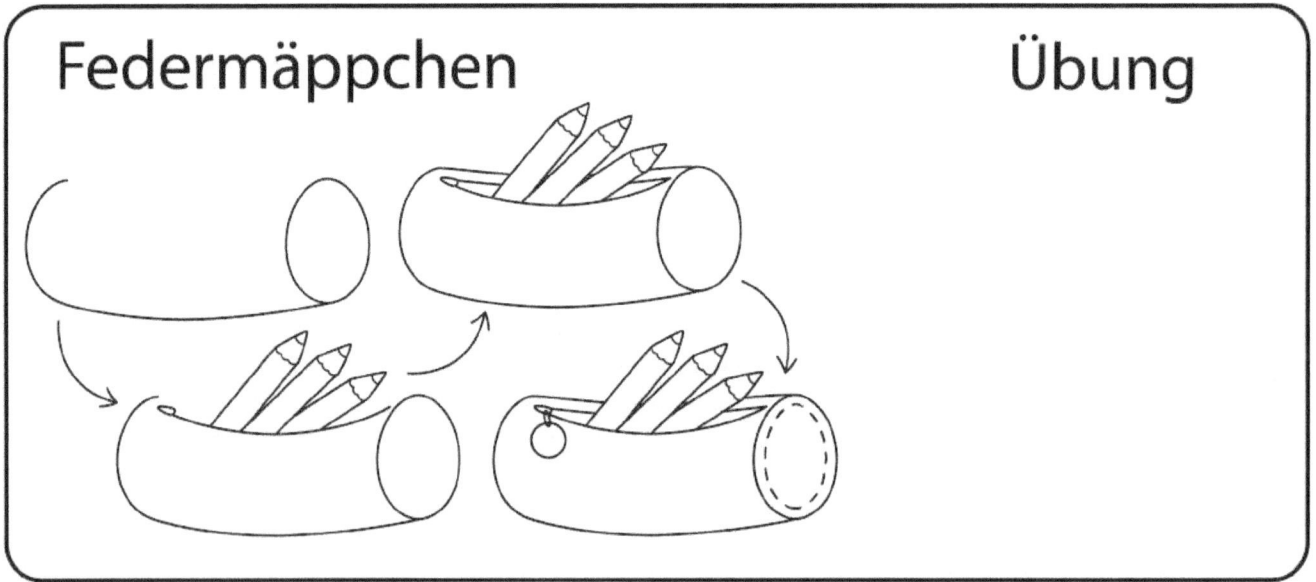

Kunst und Handwerk

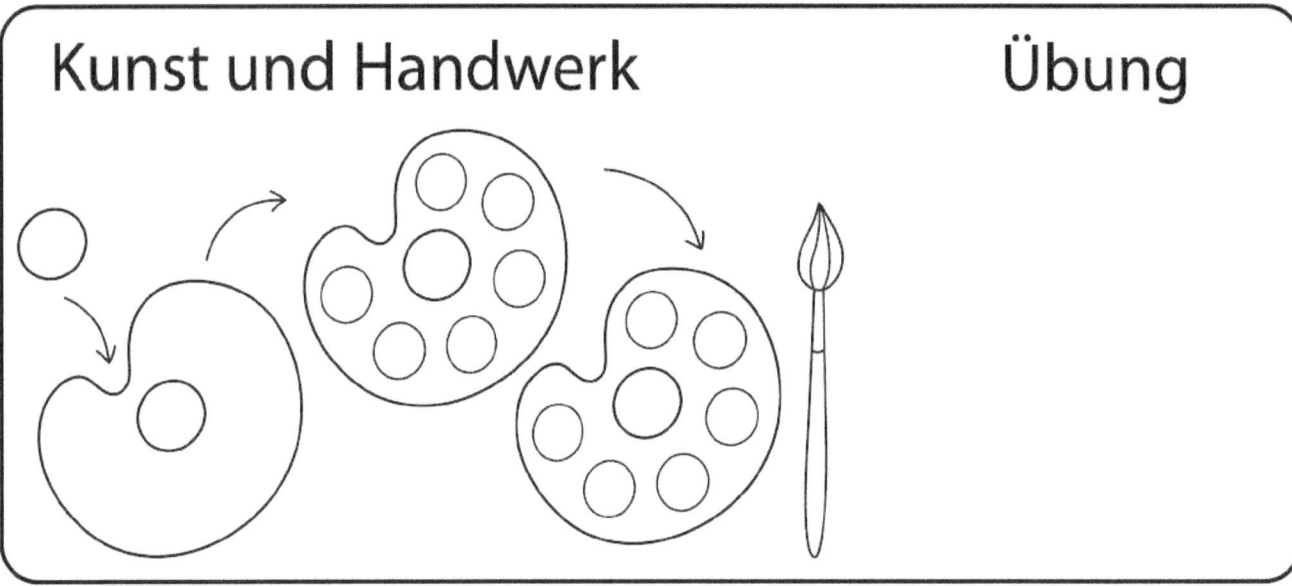

Trennwände

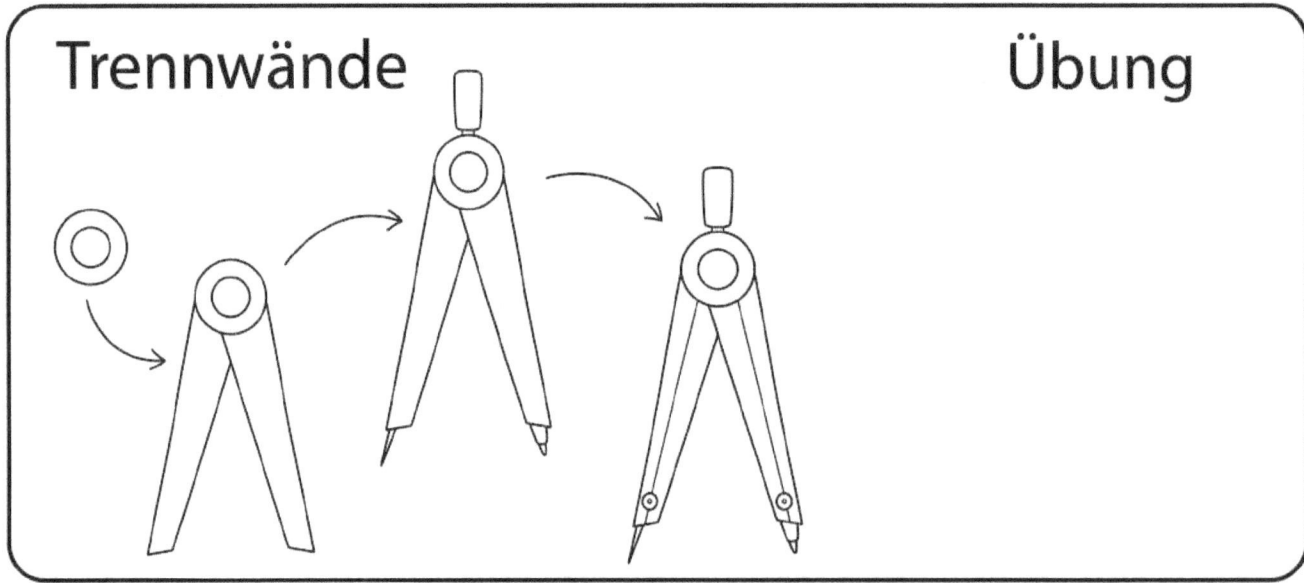

Schulranzen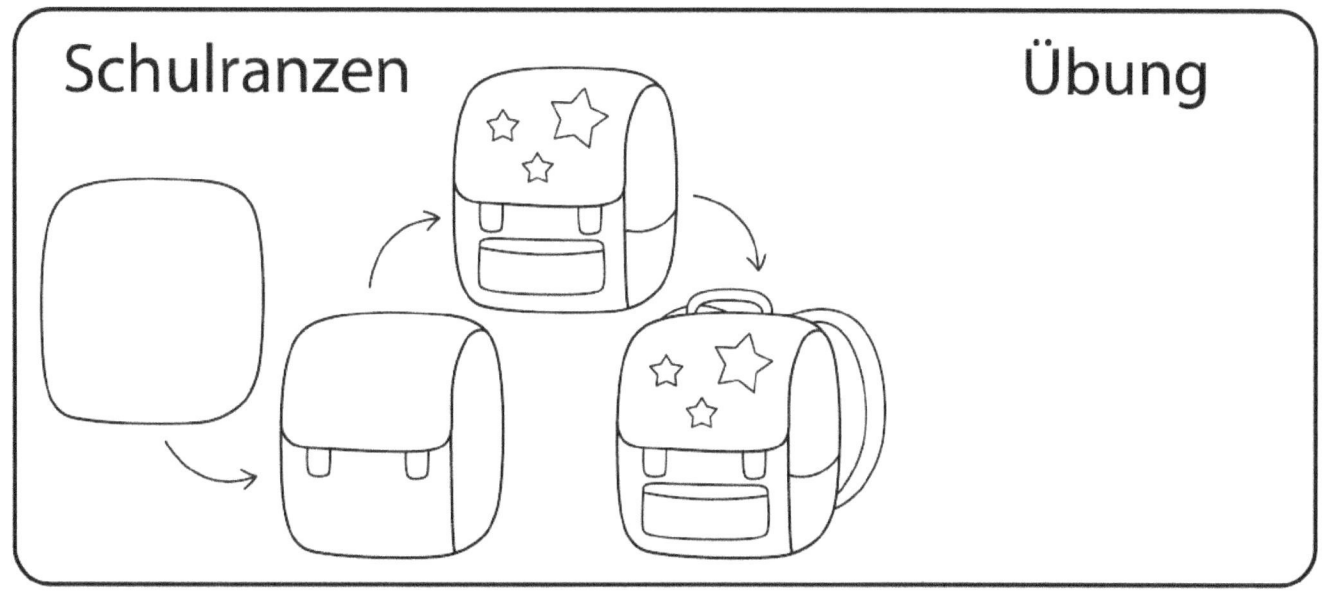

Wecker

Whiteboard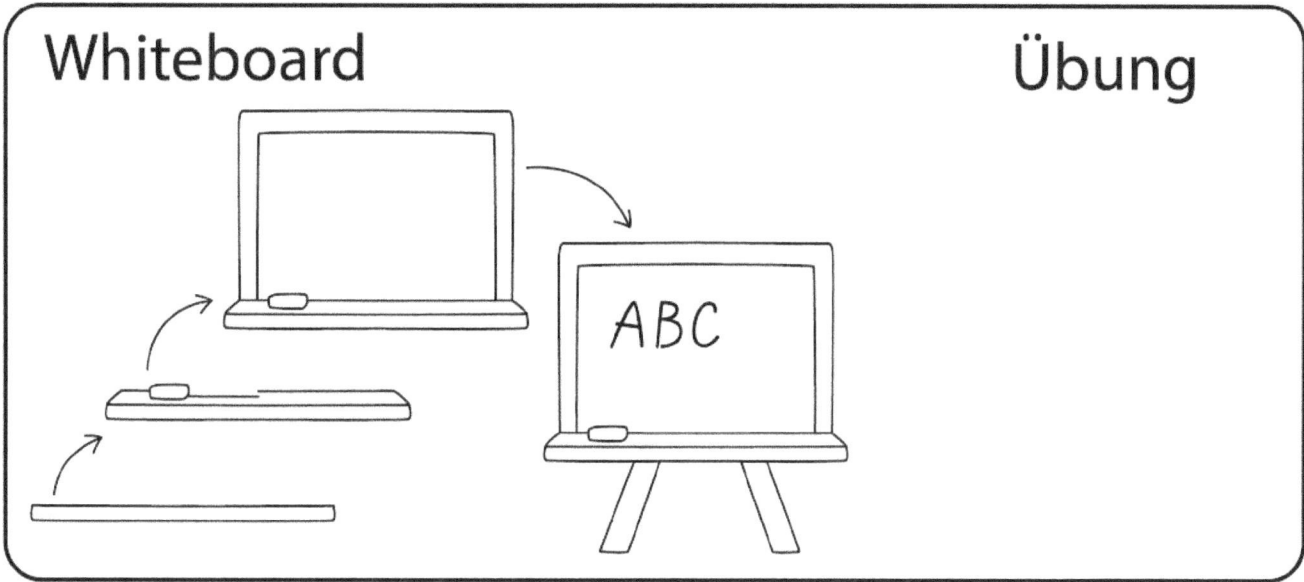

Mikrofon Übung

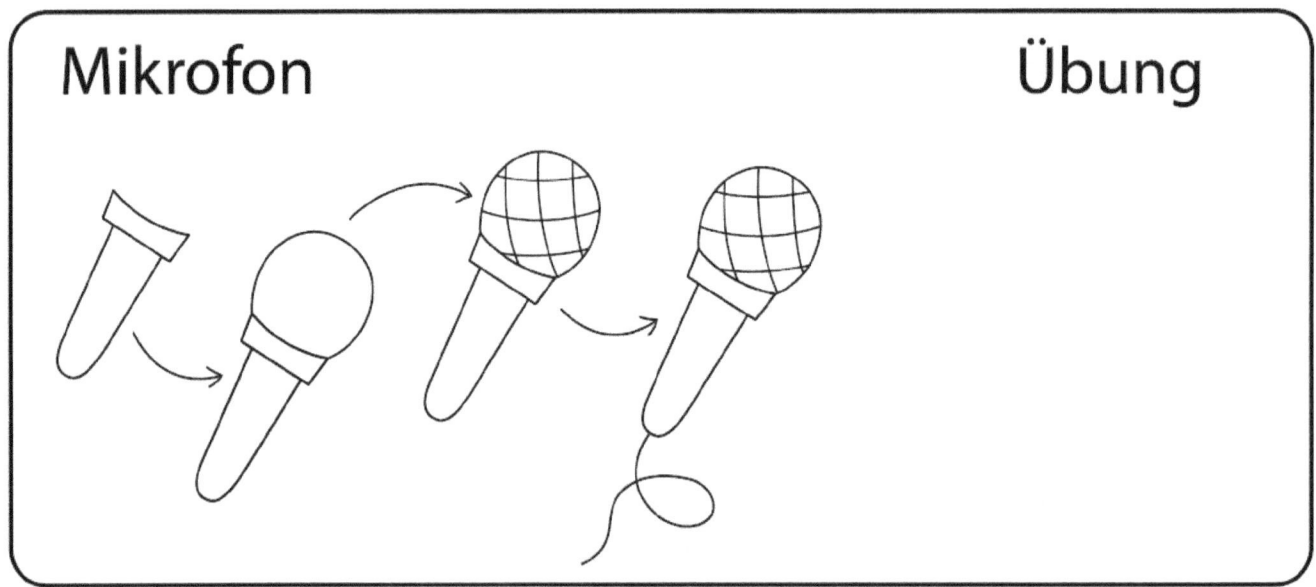

Schlagzeug Übung

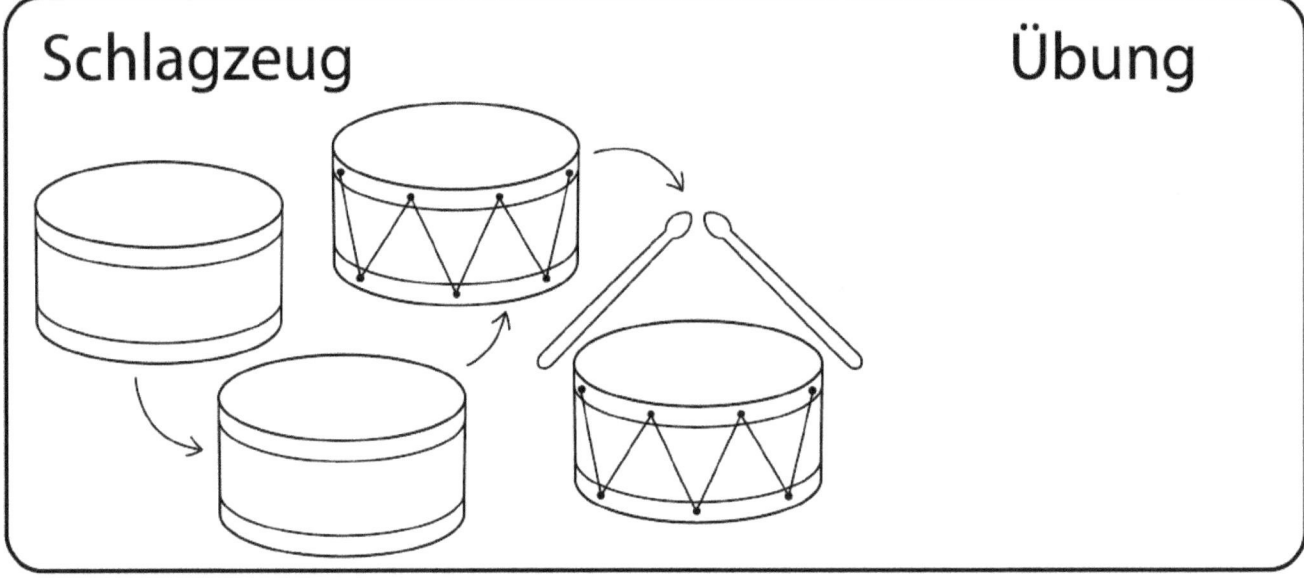

Klavier Übung

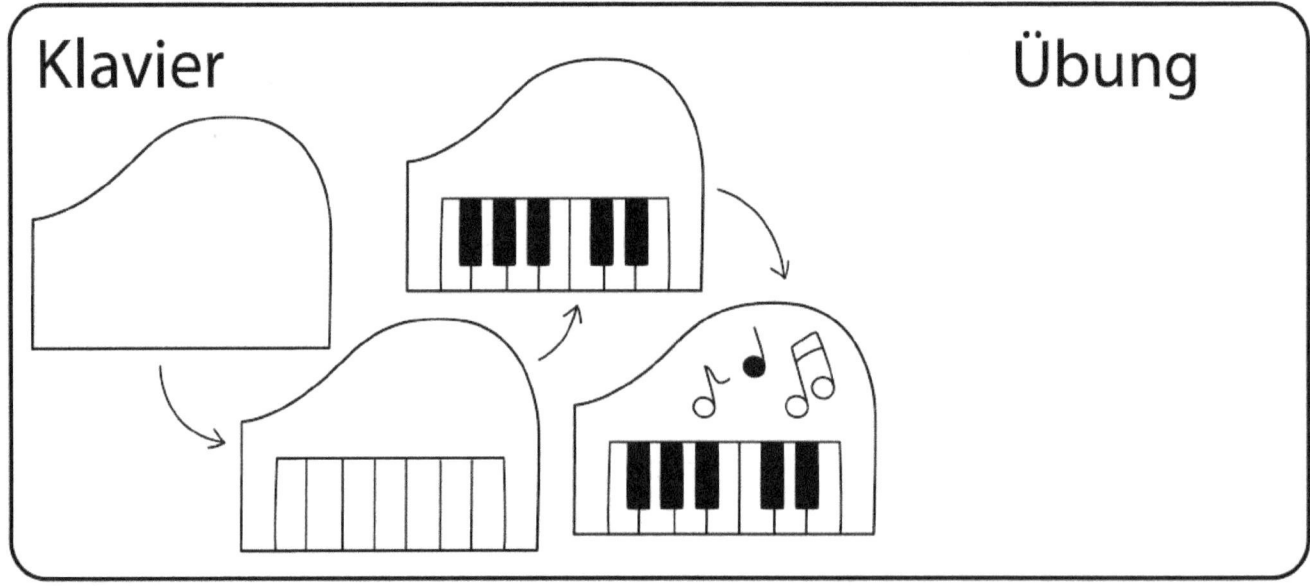

Rollschuhe Übung

Schlittschuhe Übung

Skateboard Übung

Volleyball Übung

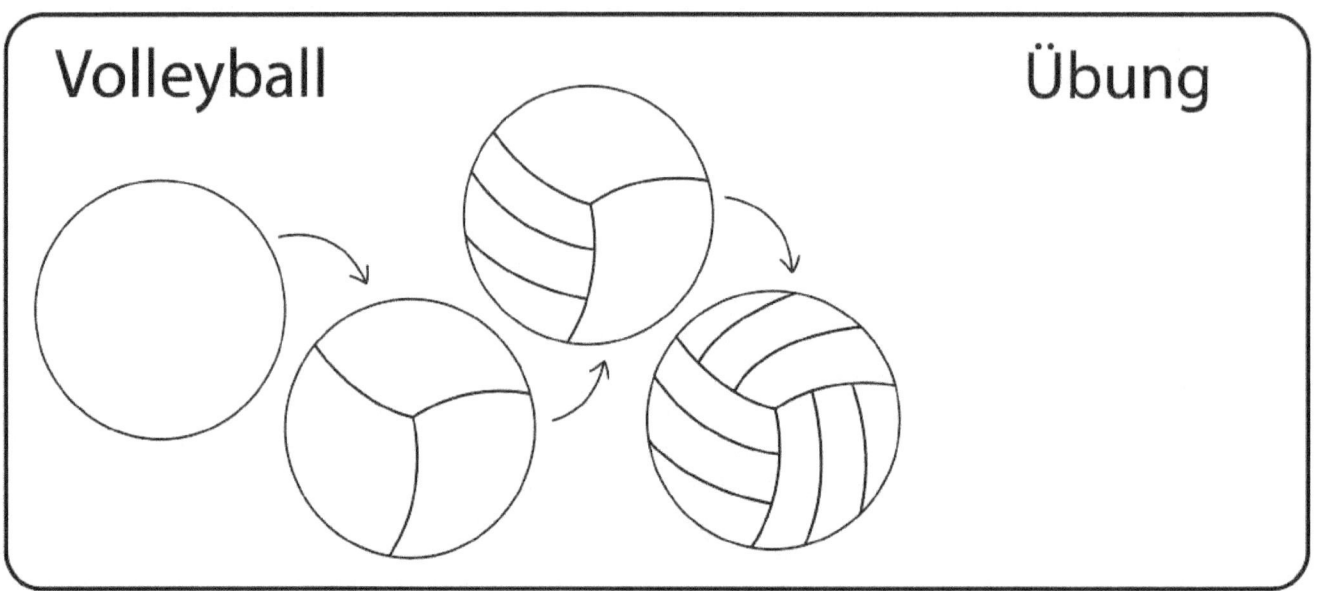

Fußball Übung

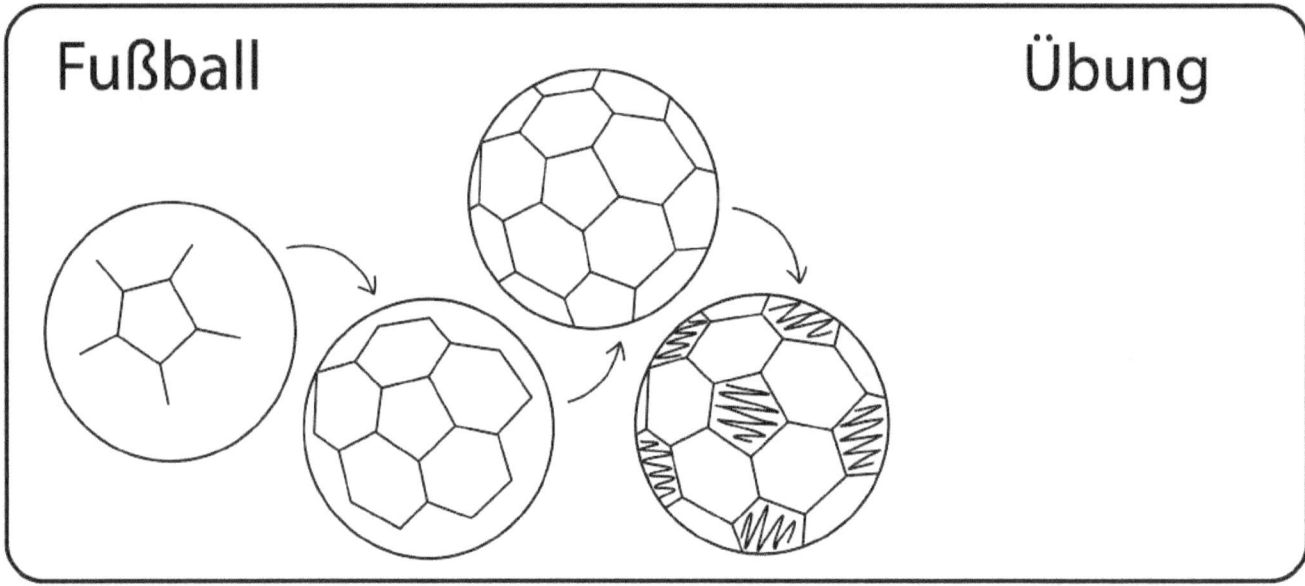

Football Übung

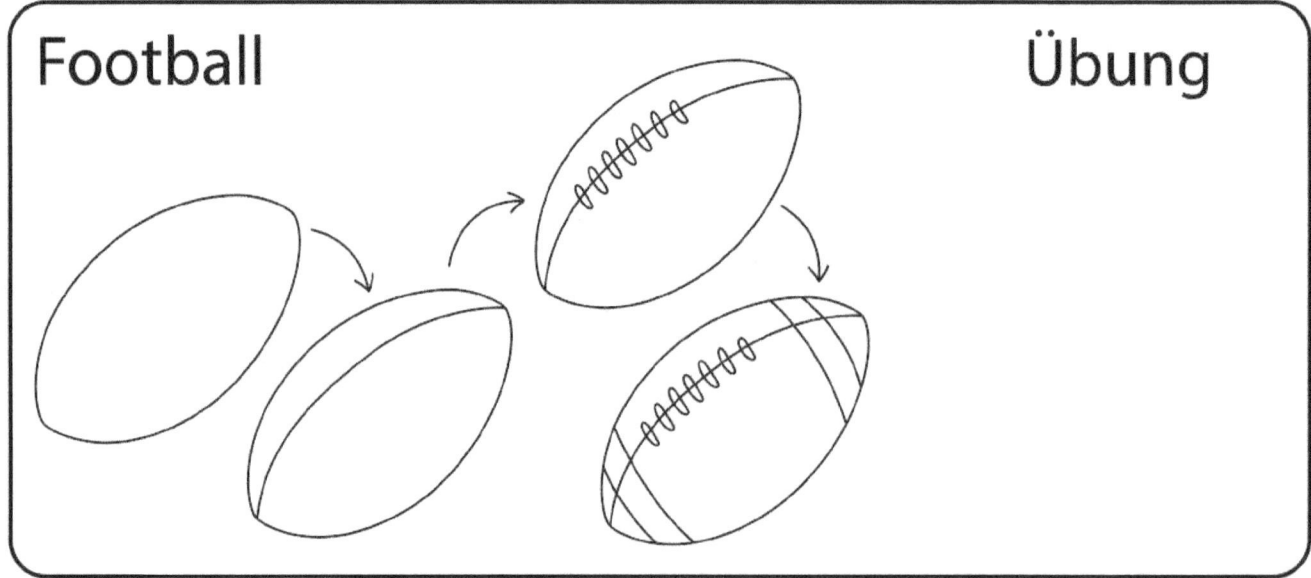

Basketball

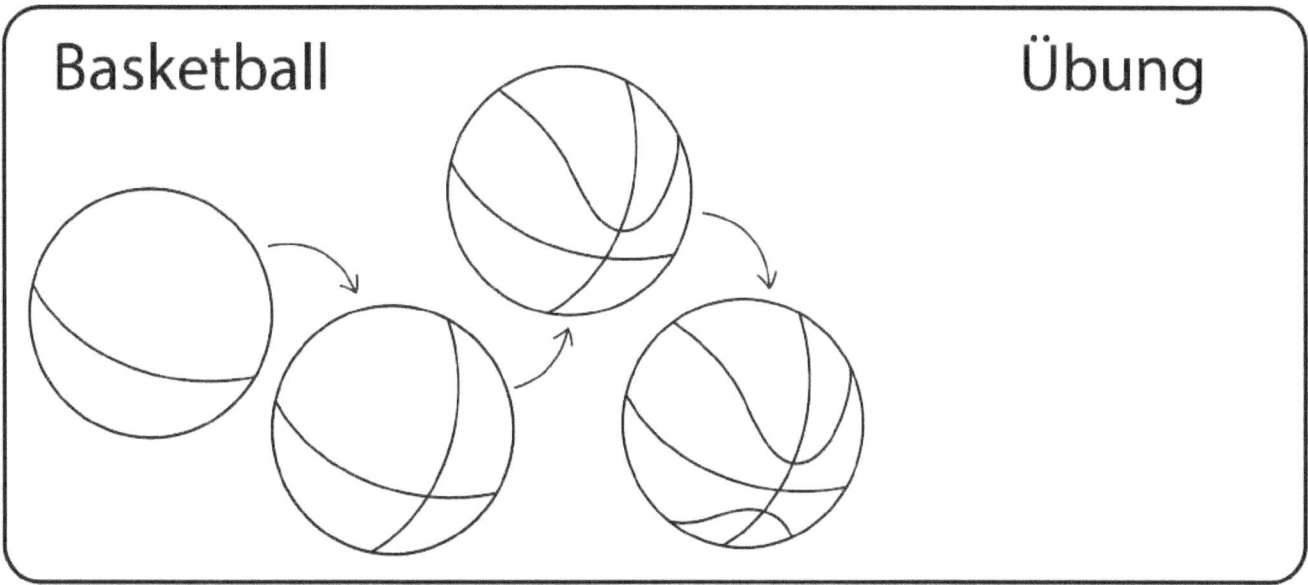

Pokal

Boxhandschuhe

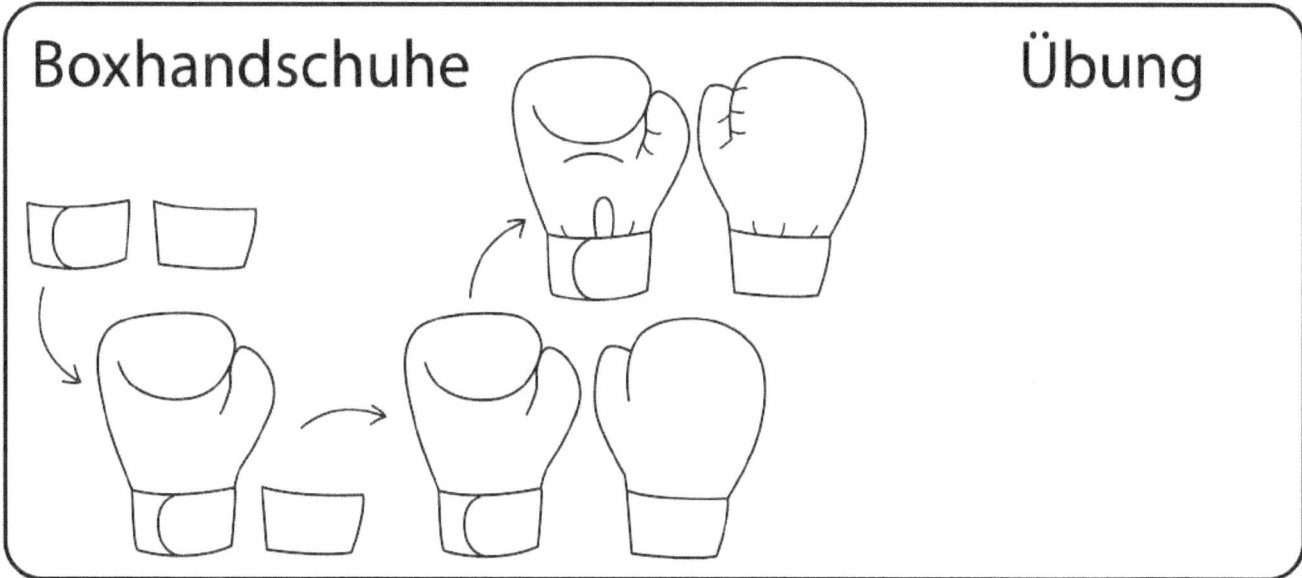

Lachendes Gesicht   Übung

Überraschtes Gesicht   Übung

Weinendes Gesicht   Übung

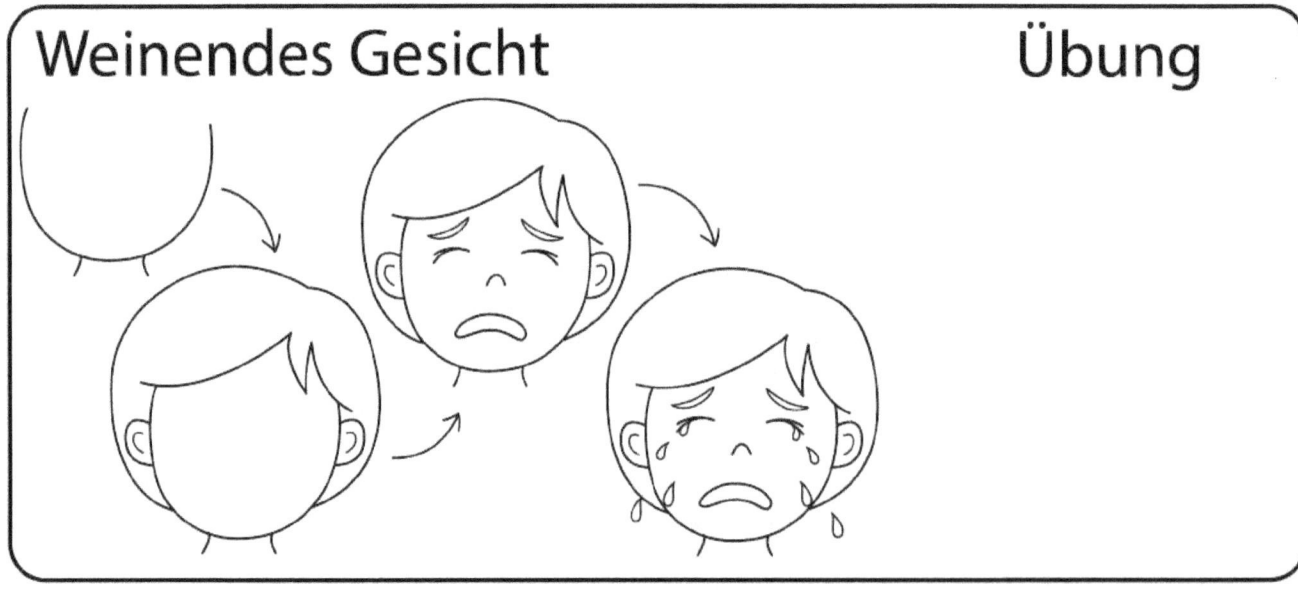

Lächelndes Gesicht Übung

Wütendes Gesicht Übung

Albernes Gesicht Übung

Cheeseburger Übung

Hotdog Übung

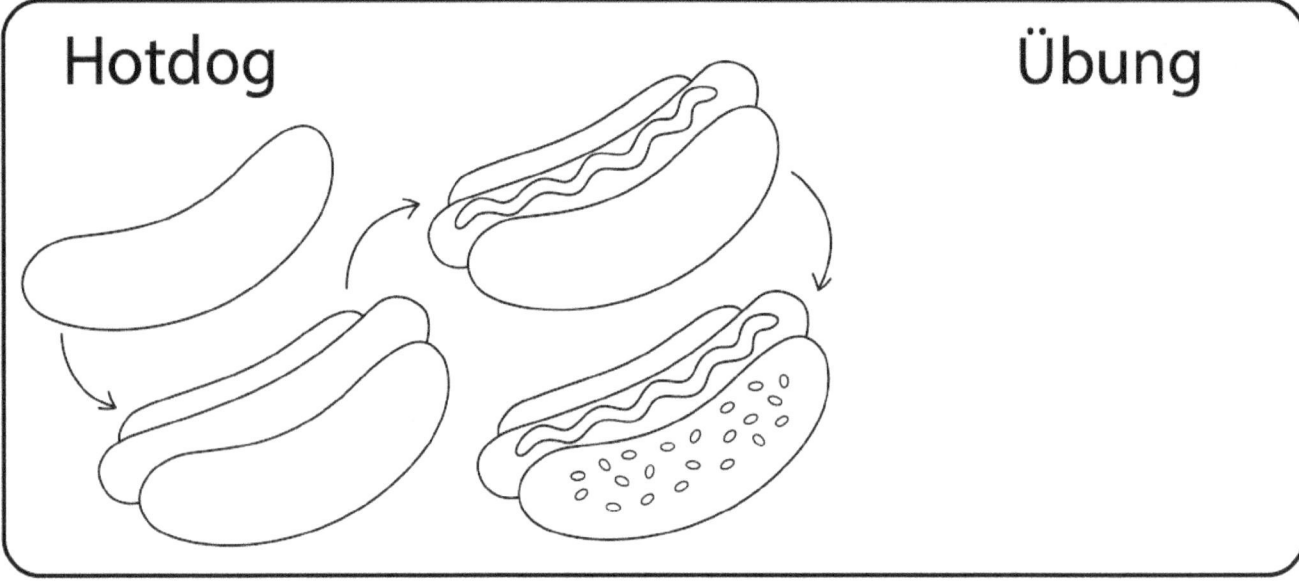

Pizza Übung

Karotte Übung

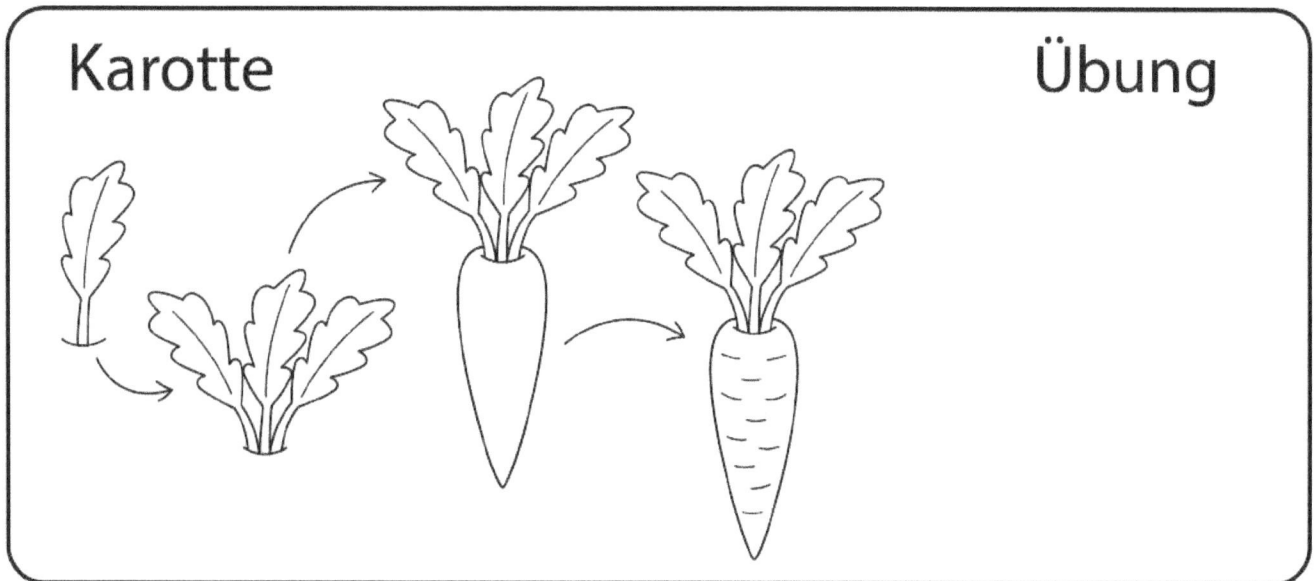

Brokkoli Übung

Erdbeere Übung

www.puzzlepalsbooks.com/kids

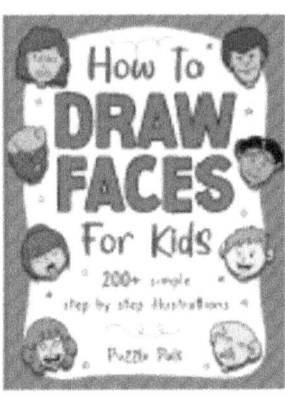

@puzzlepals_books

puzzlepalsbooks